BKN 7/ACH

# DIGGING UP THE BIBLE LANDS

A BODLEY HEAD ARCHAEOLOGY

# Digging up the Bible Lands

RONALD HARKER

*Drawings by*
MARTIN SIMMONS

THE BODLEY HEAD · London Sydney Toronto

UNIFORM WITH THIS BOOK

MAGNUS MAGNUSSON *Introducing Archaeology*
T. G. H. JAMES *The Archaeology of Ancient Egypt*

IN PREPARATION

REYNOLD HIGGINS *Minoan Crete*
HUMPHREY CASE *The Dawn of European Civilisation*
MAGNUS MAGNUSSON *Viking Expansion Westwards*

FRONTISPIECE
The three levels of
Herod the Great's
pleasure palace on the
northern tip of
Masada

© Ronald Harker, 1972
Drawings © The Bodley Head Ltd 1972
ISBN 0 370 01569 X
Printed and bound in Great Britain for
The Bodley Head Ltd
9 Bow Street, London WC2E 7AL
by William Clowes & Sons Ltd, Beccles
Set in Monophoto Ehrhardt by
BAS Printers Limited, Wallop, Hampshire
*First published 1972*

# CONTENTS

# ACKNOWLEDGMENTS

I acknowledge my grateful thanks to my wife, and to my friends Yigael and Carmella Yadin, Mrs Harry Sacher, and Hyam and Doris Morrison, for their help and encouragement.

Thanks are due to the following for permission to reproduce black and white photographs: Philipp Giegel, Zurich, frontispiece; Dr K. M. Kenyon and the Jericho Excavation Fund, pages 13, 50, 52, 54, 55, 57; The Trustees of the British Museum, pages 16, 25, 26, 28, 30, 32, 43, 45; The Mansell Collection pages, 19, 20, 36, 39, 42; *The Observer* newspaper, pages 21, 76, 82, 86, 87, 91; Dr K. M. Kenyon and the Jerusalem Excavation Fund, pages 61, 67; *The Times* newspaper, page 72; Professor Yigael Yadin, pages 97, 98, 100, 102, 105, 106, 107; Dr John Allegro, pages 110, 113, 116, 119, 121, 122.

Thanks are due to the following for permission to reproduce coloured photographs: The Trustees of the British Museum, facing page 48 (*top* and *bottom*); Middle East Archive, facing page 49; the Defence Ministry of Israel, facing pages 64, 65 (*bottom*); Dr K. M. Kenyon and the Jerusalem Excavation Fund, facing page 65 (*top*); Philipp Giegel, Zurich, facing page 80; *The Observer* newspaper, facing pages 81, 96; Professor Yigael Yadin, facing page 97.

The plan on page 70 is based on one appearing in *Jerusalem* by Dr K.M. Kenyon (Thames and Hudson); the plan on page 90 is based on one appearing in *Masada* by Professor Yigael Yadin (Weidenfeld and Nicolson), and the plan on page 99 is based on one appearing in *Bar Kokhba* by Professor Yigael Yadin (Weidenfeld and Nicolson).

# PREFACE

It is often asked whether the scholar or the amateur is best equipped to convey to the lay reader the facts and drama of scientific discovery. There is no doubt in my mind that Ronald Harker's book is a fine example of the latter's preference, but then he is perhaps particularly competent; for not only is it his profession to convey and interpret data, and not only does he love the Bible, but he has personally and closely followed the excavations of Masada and other discoveries in Biblical lands.

When we hear from time to time of a new discovery which increases our knowledge of the Biblical lands and their peoples, we often forget that many of the great discoveries were already made one hundred years ago, by devoted—albeit sometimes amateur—men. A fascinating aspect, therefore, of this book, is the space devoted and the admiration expressed by Harker to the early pioneers, followed by the most recent discoveries in the Holy Land.

Straightforward reporting, interwoven with poetic style, make this book very readable and instructive. Surely it must whet the appetite of anyone who reads it to delve more deeply into these subjects.

YIGAEL YADIN

# INTRODUCTION

In the foundations of a nineteenth-century building demolished in London some years ago the workmen found a cylinder containing a copy of *The Times* newspaper, a newly-minted penny, the names of prominent citizens who had watched the interment, and one or two other commonplace items in use at the time the building was new. It has been a fashionable way for one generation to send signals to the future. The things had little value. It is as difficult for us to guess what will be of most interest to unborn generations as it is to conceive which of the things we use will seem of least value to them. Occasionally some hoard of gold or gems, buried for a far different reason, falls into our hands to tell us how our ancestors lived and adorned themselves; and there are the decayed and lost things for which the owners perhaps had little regard, but which have more information for our own time than either buried wealth or secreted mementos. The skin of the earth is a safe deposit of history's trash and treasure, and those parts of the earth where man has lived most intensely are what draw the archaeologist to find both.

There is no richer field for the archaeologist than the Middle East—that expanse of land between Orient and Occident where art, and science and religious belief set patterns for Western civilisation. The Bible is unique among written records of early times in this part of the world. Jews and Christians for a long time accepted the Old and New Testaments as literal history. Scholars and archaeologists have much modified these convictions. Few now, for example, believe the seventeenth-century assertion of Archbishop Ussher that the creation of the world as described in the Book of Genesis happened during the week ending October 23, in the year 4004 BC.

Many scholars now question the uniqueness of the Christian ethic.

Not surprisingly the confirmation or correction of the Bible as history has been a prime objective of archaeology. The Bible and the history of Jewry are both marked with events which can be checked with other sources, and places whose remains can be identified.

There follows in this book a sequence of archaeological exploration of outstanding places and events spanning the story of Jewry and the birth of Christianity from the Biblical beginnings to the last attempt of the Jews to re-establish an Israelite nation-state. These are: discoveries related to the Biblical origins and early history of the Jewish people; Jericho and its capture by Joshua as a prelude to the establishment of the first sovereign State of Israel; Jerusalem, whose chequered story covers nearly 5,000 years; a major effort by the Jews to establish a new Israel after the crucifixion of Christ; their last bid to break their thralldom to Rome; and the discovery of writings of a Dead Sea sect of Jesus's time which in 1972 had still not been fully investigated.

# 1

# From the Beginning

The Jewish people, who are to be found in all parts of the world today, began their recorded wanderings in Iraq. The Old Testament of the Bible is a chronicle of their travels, tribulations and triumphs, but it is not a log book in the ordinary sense, setting events down in the way and order in which they happened. It is rather a collection of religious testimonies by a people who believed their god was the one and only God, and who related their experiences to his approval or disapproval of their behaviour. This is not to say, however, that the chronicles are without historical base.

They say that the ancestor of the Jews was Terah and that he set out with his family from a city called Ur of the Chaldees in Mesopotamia for a place called Haran. The site of Haran has been found in the mountains of south-east Turkey, and so have the remains of Ur, six hundred miles away, a city which modern excavations suggest may be more than 6,000 years old. Terah's descendants are named in the Bible as Abraham, his son Isaac, and his grandson Jacob; and the Jews call these men the Patriarchs. The Book of Genesis reports that when Abraham was dying—probably not far from Hebron in southern Judea, where his body was later entombed —he spoke of his native place as Nahor, and archaeologists have found Nahor, too, not far from Haran.

No precise point of time or place can be fixed for the origin of any people. Like others, the Jews were nomadic folk, moving with their flocks as the seasons and their instincts guided them. About 4,000 years ago a number of them, led by Abraham, made their way into Palestine, which the Bible calls Canaan, and later, perhaps driven by drought in search of more fertile land, they reached Egypt.

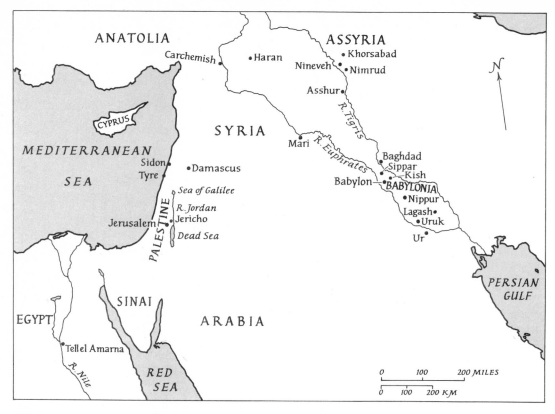

The Ancient
Near East

There they began a more settled existence. They grew in numbers, so much so that the Egyptians began to fear that as a close-knit alien community they might become dangerous; and yet the Egyptian Pharaoh was reluctant to expel them and so deprive himself of a supply of cheap labour and the revenue from the heavy taxes he made them pay. A breaking point seems to have come in the thirteenth century BC: the Jews decided to end their bondage and, now led by Moses, they trekked out of Egypt and camped in Sinai, the vast triangle of desert pointing into the Red Sea between Egypt and Arabia. This was the Exodus.

The trekkers moved slowly back towards Canaan, the country that they claimed had long ago been promised by God to Abraham 'for an everlasting possession' as a land flowing with milk and honey. This promise, the Bible says, was renewed to Abraham's son and grandson, and then, after forty years of hardship in the wilderness, to Moses. Moses himself was permitted to see the Promised Land only from afar off, looking westward across the River Jordan as he lay dying in the mountains of Moab. 'I am 120 years old this day,' Moses says in the Book of Deuteronomy. 'I can no more go out and

The site of ancient
Jericho after
excavation.

come in. Also the Lord hath said unto me thou shalt not go over this
Jordan.' Instead, he told his people the Lord had declared, 'Joshua,
he shall go over before thee.'

So Joshua took command. The trekkers crossed the River Jordan
opposite the walled Canaanite settlement of Jericho, where the waters
of an oasis created—and still mark—a sharp contrast between luxurious green growth and the desert wastes that now lay behind the Jews.
Joshua took Jericho by stratagem and storm, and so opened a campaign of conquest. The Jews settled in the hills of Samaria and
Judea in family tribes: the Bible says there were twelve of them, but
they were not united until threats by the Philistines from the coastal
region in the west drove them into a defensive union. The small
Benjamite tribe produced a clever guerrilla leader in Saul, and the
other tribes were so impressed by his successes that they made him
their first king. He was, however, less successful as a king than as
a roving warrior, and at length the powerful priest and prophet
Samuel decided Saul was unreliable. He picked on the young,
handsome, and brave ex-shepherd David, who was Saul's armour-
bearer and had become a hero in his own right by his triumph in a
duel with the Philistine champion, Goliath. Samuel was sure David
would make a better king. Saul in the end made the mistake of
challenging the better-armed Philistines in open battle and went
down to defeat on the mountains of Gilboa. Unable to bear the

13

shame and misery of it, he asked his sword-bearer to kill him, and it was to David that the southern tribes first, and then the northern tribes, turned for leadership. David completed the work which had been beyond the capacity of Saul: he turned the loose confederation of family tribes, for their own security, into a national state—the state of Israel.

Among their own settlements remained one point hostile to them all—the city of Jerusalem, held by older inhabitants of Canaan, called Jebusites. David laid siege to Jerusalem and captured it much as Joshua before him had captured Jericho, by guile and assault. He made it his capital because of its central position among the tribes, and brought to it the Ark of the Covenant. The Ark was the Jews' sacred object representing God and his covenant or pledge to them of his fatherly concern. It was a wooden chest overlaid with gold and its presence implied victory for the Israelites. So the priests carried it into battle on poles thrust through rings in its sides. If others touched it, this was a desecration punishable by death, and indeed once, when it was captured by the Philistines, they ascribed to it their subsequent ill-luck and sent it back to the Israelites.

With the Ark of the Covenant in Jerusalem the city became a religious as well as political capital. And there David's most famous son Solomon built the first Temple to the one god of the Jews 3,000 years ago. It was the biggest place of worship in Canaan, its complex of buildings covering a greater area than London's St Paul's Cathedral, and it dominated Jerusalem on its hilltop site.

Solomon ruled in splendour until 928 BC. After his death the Hebrews split into two kingdoms: ten of the tribes in the north, which was bigger, richer and more fertile, deserted the dynasty of David but kept the name of Israel, leaving the heirs of Solomon with the small southern, and poorer, portion of Judah, the rump of his old tribal territory. But Judah had the advantage of containing the religious focal point of Jerusalem, whilst Israel had to find a new capital, and so built Samaria in the mountains of Ephraim.

The two sides fought each other spasmodically for the next two centuries, until another people, the Assyrians from the north-east (where the Jews' own ancestors had come from), advanced upon the northern kingdom. The Israelites resisted. One of their leaders, King Ahab, is said to have commanded 2,000 chariots and 10,000 infantry, and with local allies his army held up the invasion. Warfare was protracted. One Assyrian king undertook sixteen campaigns, and more than a hundred years went by before the aggressors were

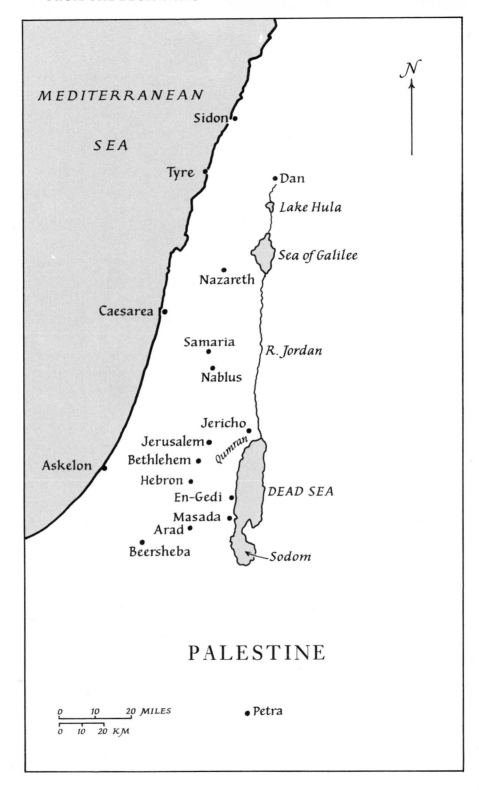

PALESTINE

able to turn the northern kingdom into a province of their empire. They captured King Hoshea, the last King of Israel, outside his capital of Samaria.

The Assyrians carried off the chief citizens, and they vanish from history. The remainder, the poor and unimportant, married with foreign settlers brought (says the Book of Kings) from other parts of the Assyrian empire, and from this intermingling sprang the Samaritans. These keep their separate identity to this day; a few families still live in Shechem, now called Nablus, claiming that their religious beliefs represent the true teaching of Moses, the only prophet they recognise.

Like all conquerors, the Assyrians in time declined in power. The contenders for their empire were Babylonia in the north-east and Egypt in the south-west. Judah, lying between them, was crushed in the struggle. The Babylonians were led by King Nebuchadrezzar; he captured Jerusalem in 586 BC, burned it to the ground, and carried off the most important Jews, just as the Assyrians had done from Israel. This was the end of Judah.

It was not, of course, the end of the Jews. Throughout their captivity the exiles in Babylon kept their faith and somehow kept contact with the rest of their kin left behind in Judah. Cyrus the Persian conquered Babylon in 538 BC, and he allowed the exiled Jews to return. Their prophet Jeremiah had forecast that their captivity would last seventy years, and in 516 BC, exactly seventy years after their deportation, they completed the rebuilding of their Temple in Jerusalem. They also brought back strict observance of their ancient laws. Two of their leaders, Ezra, a priest who was living in the fifth century BC, and Nehemiah, barred their people

On this clay cylinder found at Babylon Cyrus records his defeat of King Nabonidus and his conquest of Babylon. He also tells how he restored to their original shrines images of gods which had been collected by Nabonidus.

16

from marrying outside the faith, and so gave the Jews one element of exclusiveness the more orthodox among them have kept ever since.

It is now generally believed that the Jews began setting down their story around David's time, or about 1000 BC. They were still compiling their chronicles five hundred years later on their return from Babylonian exile, and this is where the Old Testament ends. But their homecoming brought them no lasting liberty: they had to suffer a succession of other masters—Persians, Macedonians, Egyptians again, and Syrians. Then, in the second century BC, a noble Jewish family, the Maccabees, rallied the Jewish people, and for a short spell they enjoyed independence under Maccabean rule. But again it was not to last. Family quarrels broke out among the Maccabees themselves and this time a new expansionist power in the ancient world intervened. Roman legions came from Italy. Their commander, Pompey, then empire-building in Syria, saw the opportunity offered by Palestine's internal strife, and marched south. He laid siege to Jerusalem in 63 BC and took it after three months, massacring the inhabitants. Thereafter the Romans ruled Palestine through puppet kings, the most notable of whom was Herod the Great. He was appointed by the Roman Senate in 40 BC to be King of Judea.

Roman coin of
Pompey

Herod, who was himself of Arab stock, was unable to reconcile Romans and Jews. Anxious to keep on good terms with both, he sacrificed to the Romans' pagan gods, but rebuilt the Temple for the Jews even more magnificently than Solomon. But he also ordered his secret police to seize troublemakers, especially Jewish would-be freedom-fighters, and he put suspects to death in fortress prisons all over the land. Herod died in 4 BC, and the Romans then appointed their own governors in Palestine.

It was not an easy part of their empire to rule. Jews were excused military service because they objected to the legions' continuous contact with idolatry (vessels required for sacrifices were part of Roman army equipment, even on active service). The Roman soldiers began to leave their standards in their barracks when they marched past the Temple, to avoid the risk of offending the touchy Jews by flaunting these pagan symbols. Pontius Pilate was procurator of Judea between 26 and 36 AD, and when he broke this courtesy custom there was a riot in Jerusalem. Pilate saw Jesus as a troublesome subject, but when he surrendered him to the ortho-dox Jews as a dangerous heretic it was also the kind of diplomatic

Roman coin of
Vespasian

Roman coin of Titus

step that Rome's representative felt obliged to make. In fact, after
the execution of Jesus, Rome specifically ordered its officials to deal
leniently with the Jews, and when Pilate forcibly dispersed a religious
gathering on Mount Gerizim north of Jerusalem, he was summoned
to Rome and dismissed.

But hostility continued to build up, fed by the Emperor Nero's
importation of Greek, that is, pagan, practices, a corrupt local
administration, and trouble-making by Jewish nationalists known
as Zealots. Then, when the Governor Gessius Florus demanded
money from the Temple treasury, the Jews refused, and in 66 AD
exploded in revolt. Nero sent his general Vespasian and an army
60,000 strong to quell it. In a few months he subdued all Galilee, and
by the spring of 69 AD he had encircled the remaining defiant
nationalists in the Jerusalem district and in a few forts near the Dead
Sea. Nero had taken his own life the previous summer, and the army
elected Vespasian as the new Emperor. He left his son Titus to
finish the subjection of Palestine. Titus set up his headquarters on a
ridge north-east of Jerusalem called Mount Scopus (because from
it one can *scan* the whole city—the same word as in 'telescope')
and watched his siege engines batter down the northern walls. In
70 AD the city was sacked and the Temple destroyed.

The Jews were, of course, no match for the Roman soldiery in
pitched battle, but as history up to our own times has shown—in
Algeria, Malaysia, Vietnam—big battalions alone cannot easily defeat determined and dedicated guerrillas in their native land. At the
start of the rebellion, in 66 AD, the Jews in the south had taken
the Romans by surprise and massacred their local garrison on the
towering rock of Masada on the western shores of the Dead Sea.
Now a group of fanatical Jewish Zealots escaped from Jerusalem
and joined these last rebels in the wilderness of Judea. Together
they held out for another three years. Their situation, however,
became more and more desperate, and when the Romans surrounded
the rock with a wall and eight siege camps, it became hopeless.
As the Tenth Legion commanded by Flavius Silva stormed the cliff-
tops, the Jews made a last tragic gesture of defiance and contempt
by setting fire to the fortress and taking their own lives.

Sixty years later, in 132 AD, the Jews made one more bid for
freedom under the guerrilla leader Shimon bar Kokhba in a two-and-
a-half-year war even bloodier than that of 66–73 AD. Hundreds of
thousands of Jews are believed to have died in battle, and tens of
thousands were sold abroad as slaves or sent to their deaths in Roman

Silver coin of Bar
Kokhba inscribed 'of
the Freedom of
Jerusalem'

A *bas relief* from the Arch of Titus in Rome shows his soldiers carrying off sacred vessels from the Temple during the sack of Jerusalem.

circuses. The rest—or many of them—scattered. This was the beginning of the Diaspora, the great dispersion. Eighteen centuries went by before Jewish settlers, fighting off attack by five Arab armies, re-established a sovereign State of Israel in May 1948.

This is the brief historical background to the long story of the Jews which scholars have been able to piece together from many sources and the chronicles of many other peoples. One of the most fascinating sources has been archaeology—the digging up of buried history. Over the past 150 years archaeology has done a great deal to illuminate the world of the Bible, sometimes reinforcing the written records, sometimes correcting them, but always bringing closer the past as it really was.

Today the Israelis, like all new nations, have taken fresh interest in their own early history and have made spectacularly successful excavations. The impulse to excavate in the Bible lands, however, was pioneered in the Middle East not by the Jews themselves but by Europeans and Americans. Up to a century ago knowledge of history in the Bible lands was limited to scholars, and even they had only the Bible itself for sources earlier than five or six hundred years before Christ. Then, in the nineteenth century, there arose a desire to try to confirm Biblical history. Public interest grew with the discoveries of men who were consuls or political officers in the Middle East, and to whom archaeology was a hobby born of personal curiosity. Their methods were amateur, sometimes disastrous, and usually limited by shortage of means. In rugged and difficult con-

19

Early expeditions took away their finds to enrich their own national or private collections. An illustration from Sir Henry Layard's book *Nineveh and its Remains*, showing his removal of Assyrian sculptures for the British Museum. The mound of Nimrud is in the background.

ditions, often set upon and robbed by bandits, helped only by handfuls of local workers who might quit in the middle of an excavation (and even in the middle of the night) those lonely, dedicated men pursued their interest with astonishing zeal and courage. Their rewards were great, and sometimes greater than they lived to know. Slowly their discoveries roused world interest, and this had two results—one of incalculable loss, the other of immeasurable value.

Apart from a few outstanding men and women, the first diggers were looters. The more sophisticated were like the men who transported the obelisks called Cleopatra's Needles from Heliopolis in Egypt to New York and the Thames Embankment. The more ignorant and vastly more numerous vandals were local peasantry, quick to see the opportunity for profit from foreign avarice, and this has continued ever since. In Turkey today country folk have used dynamite on suspected ancient sites, and bulldozed hilltops that looked like, and often were, ancient burial grounds in pursuit of easy plunder.

The second and fruitful consequence of the world's awakening interest has been the appearance of the modern archaeologist as a trained investigator. He may still find rich royal tombs and hoards of treasure, but he spends most of his time unearthing, classifying and interpreting things of little or no value in themselves. He is looking for artifacts—the word used for anything made by man, however humble. These are prized as keys to the understanding of ancient human life.

When an artifact is found in a layer of earth, and there are similar artifacts or records of them elsewhere of a known date, then habitation of the earth layer can be dated and the kind of people who lived there is known. Among artifacts, archaeologists most value pottery fragments, because they are almost indestructible and provide guidelines to the growth of civilisation as shown in man's changing tastes and skills. Nowadays the archaeologist has all kinds of scientific and mechanical advantages over the early pioneers. Instead of trekking on foot with primitive tools loaded (in the case of desert exploration) on camels or donkeys he naturally uses motor transport. Canned and frozen foods and water pumped by pipeline have diminished the problem of supplies. But the more significant change is of method. Where the pioneers were keen amateurs from the educated few, relying heavily on applied intuition in picking a site for digging, the modern professional starts off with aerial survey by telescopic camera, plotting the prospective area of search on a grid system. Instead of

Much of the work in the 1963–65 excavations at Masada was done by volunteers. Modern expedition leaders have found helpers of this kind, enthusiastic and mostly young, preferable to hiring unskilled, and mostly indifferent, local labour.

sinking shafts with little more than the hope of a lucky strike, he trenches systematically. For dating he has the help of carbon tests of age which are a by-product of atomic research.

One change, however, that seems not to fit with these material developments is the composition of work teams. Once the archaeologist took his chance with local paid labour, which could be wasteful and disastrously clumsy through ignorance, and unreliable through disinterest. Now there is a growing habit of recruiting unpaid labour largely from the young, who are careful workers because they are informed, and diligent because their effort is volunteered. When an invitation to join an expedition to Masada was published in *The Observer* newspaper in London in 1963, it brought 5,000 applications from 28 different countries—a startling measurement of the spread of public interest in recent years.

# 2

# The Treasure
# of the River Lands

The country which our forefathers called Mesopotamia—in Greek
it means the land between rivers—is the valley of the Tigris and
Euphrates, now part of the state of Iraq. On a coloured relief map
it is a green tip to the broad blue blade of the Persian Gulf, thrusting
north-westward towards Turkey. In prehistoric times it was marsh-
land, but silt, brought down by both rivers from the mountains of
Turkish Armenia and Kurdistan, gradually filled up the marshes,
at first with islands. These became settled by primitive people who,
archaeologists have discovered, learned how to keep cattle, sheep
and goats, to grow and harvest edible grain, and—their hooks have
been found—to fish the surrounding waters.

The earliest inhabitants of whom we have any substantial knowledge were Sumerians, a people who came down from the mountain-
ous north-east and settled near the mouth of the two rivers. Quoting,
it may be, some Sumerian legend, the Bible speaks of a people who
'journeyed from the east and came into the valley of Shinar (which
is Babylon) and dwelt there.' The Sumerians founded the first
Mesopotamian civilisation more than 5,000 years ago. They developed farming methods, sculpture, painting, pottery and metal work;
they made boats and musical instruments; and by inscribing symbols on wet clay tablets, they created the world's first script.

On the heels of the Sumerians came Akkadians, who settled north
of them in the region of modern Mosul. The Akkadians were a
semitic people, an ethnic grouping probably originating in Arabia
and to which Hebrews belong. Later came other semitic tribes
migrating from infertile mountain and desert regions to the richer
soil of the river lands. The island sites spread and grew into towns

23

and then into city states, warring among themselves. Out of these petty conflicts grew empires, whose fortunes fluctuated with the appearance or absence of strong leaders. The empires that lasted longest and so left the clearer marks on human history were those of Babylon and Assyria.

Both the Babylonians and the Assyrians were bearded semitic folk who absorbed the cultures of their predecessors. They spoke the Akkadian language, but wrote in cuneiform, the script invented by the Sumerians, long after both Akkadians and Sumerians themselves had vanished from national recognition. They also inherited a common religion, expressed in a great variety of local nature gods which were credited with varying powers. Dominant gods were determined by dominant cities. Thus, when Babylon was paramount, the chief regional god was Marduk, and when Assyria was in the ascendant, the god Asshur (which was also the name of the Assyrian capital) was supreme.

Gold cups found in the Royal Cemetery at Ur.

The major seats of power in the Mesopotamian river lands at different times were the Sumerian cities of Ur, Eridu, Lagash and Nippur, the Babylonian cities of Babylon, Uruk, Kish and Sippar, the Assyrian cities of Asshur, Nineveh, and the Biblical Calah, today called locally Nimrud, and the Amorite city of Mari. Until the early nineteenth century knowledge of these cities was scanty or non-existent: the only sources of what knowledge man had were the Bible and the observations of a few Greek writers of the fifth century BC. This knowledge began to expand through archaeology, which started mainly as a fumbling pastime of inquisitive amateurs late in the eighteenth century; but during the nineteenth and twentieth centuries it developed into a science that has enabled us to redraw the map of the world of the Bible. Among the places which have yielded information about man's hidden past, none has been more rewarding than the valley of the Tigris and Euphrates, about 750 miles long and 300 miles wide. The discoveries of archaeologists there have zigzagged over time and been like pieces in some gigantic jigsaw, meaningful only when fitted into other discoveries in other places. The sites of Mesopotamia's vanished cities provided major pieces for the jigsaw picture.

## UR OF THE CHALDEES

In the Bible story the city of Ur of the Chaldees was the birth-place of Terah, the ancestor of Abraham, who led the Hebrews north-west out of the river lands to Haran, a city on the banks of a tributary of the Euphrates. From Haran Abraham and his followers turned south-westward into Egypt by way of Palestine. But when did all this happen?

Archaeologists have found from cuneiform writings that the city of Haran flourished in the nineteenth and eighteenth centuries BC. It still exists on the banks of the Balikh River, and country folk in the neighbourhood still relate legends about Abraham and regard him as a Mohammedan saint. But apart from this discovery no other evidence has been turned up that could give a verifiable date to the wanderings of the Patriarchs. To the archaeologists of the nineteenth century the key to the whole mystery seemed to be Ur of the Chaldees.

Western travellers in the seventeenth and eighteenth centuries had brought back from southern Mesopotamia copies of rock carvings they had seen but could not understand. Dr Thomas Hyde, an Oxford scholar, saw some of these in 1700 and called them 'cuneiform', meaning 'wedge-shaped'; he thought they were interesting decorations. German scholars first suggested they were an alphabet, but in the 1830s, an English officer in the East India Company, Henry Rawlinson, who had been sent to Persia as a military adviser, made a sensational break-through. On the smooth flank of a mountain called Behistun, 300 feet up from the old road linking Persia and Babylonia, he caught sight of extensive relief carvings surrounded by inscriptions. He climbed up to them and made careful copies.

Part of a page from the series *Cuneiform Inscriptions of Western Asia*, published by the British Museum under Sir Henry Rawlinson's direction after the decipherment of the script.

He felt certain the carved symbols had more significance than mere decoration; they were, in fact, cuneiform texts in Persian, Babylonian and Elamite (the three main old languages of the region) and by a long and patient process of guessing a meaning for one symbol and testing it against others, he arrived at a tentative translation of some of them into words or names. German scholars, also working on the assumption that cuneiform was syllabic writing, had already begun a similar study of the riddle, and had laboriously identified twelve, then sixteen, and eventually twenty-three symbols that made sense as letters. But Rawlinson, working quite independently, cracked the whole code. The inscription turned out to be a record of the military triumphs of Darius I, the Persian king who reigned from 521 to 486 BC.

Scholars now had a key to the hitherto locked-up secrets of the Sumerians, Akkadians, Babylonians, Assyrians, and other peoples of the Middle East, whose cultures formed the background to the Bible story. But scholars were slow to make use of the key. It was not until 1857 that conclusive proof of the decipherment of cuneiform was recognised, when four scholars were asked by Britain's Royal

The ziggurat at Ur, showing the triple staircase approach. J. E. Taylor investigated the ziggurat in 1854.

26

Asiatic Society to make independent translations of an unpublished inscription of the Assyrian king Tiglath-Pileser III, dug up at his capital at Asshur. They came up with the same result.

Three years before this, in 1854, the British vice-consul at Basra, J. E. Taylor, was asked to make a survey of southern Mesopotamia for the British Museum. When he was on the western banks of the Euphrates he examined a huge, reddish outcrop known locally as Tell Muqayyar. Apparently this curious stump was a solid pile of brickwork, and Taylor had a feeling that it was part of the ruins of Ur of the Chaldees—the Chaldeans were a semitic people of southern Babylonia. He and his party climbed the crumbling heap and demolished the top of it, searching for they knew not what. They found a few inscribed cylinders which they sent back to the British Museum. But cuneiform had not yet been definitely accepted, so the Museum simply put them away and forgot about them.

Taylor was disappointed. He thought he had found the ancient city of Ur, and he was quite right. But it was not until a joint British-American team led by Sir Charles Leonard Woolley went to Ur in 1922, nearly seventy years later, that the city itself and its treasures were uncovered. This excavation, which lasted for ten years, is one of the great 'digs' in the annals of archaeology. Unlike Taylor, Woolley did not attack the great brick mound itself but first explored the ground some distance away from it where there were signs of an ancient cemetery. And it was here that he uncovered sixteen royal graves, including one of the most spectacular death chambers ever found, made for a royal funeral dating, it is thought, from not later than 2,500 BC.

Five bodies lying side by side in a gently-sloping trench were the first warning of what lay below. Next the excavators found the bodies of ten women lying in two neat rows, wearing headdresses of gold, lapis lazuli and carnelians, and the skeleton of a musician lying across the crumbled remains of his gold-leafed harp. As the diggers worked their way down what was now clearly a ramp, they found a sledge funeral car with the skeletal remains of two grooms and two asses; six soldiers lying in two ranks, copper spears at their sides, two four-wheeled wagons with their oxen and drivers; the bodies of nine more women; and then, finally, they came to the vaulted tomb of a king of Ur and his queen Pu-abi.

The queen was dressed in jewelled and richly ornamented robes and a giant beribboned wig. Near the king were the bodies of three other people; there were 63 others in the adjacent death-pit, and

Gold jewellery from the Royal Cemetery at Ur

Headress and jewellery of gold, silver, lapis lazuli and carnelian worn by one of the women attendants in the 'Great Death Pit' at Ur.

the queen had a retinue of 21 in all.

In another death-pit were the bodies of six men servants and 68 women, all lying in regular rows, with legs slightly bent and hands brought up to the face. When a king and queen died, it obviously meant doom for the whole court, too. The oxen and asses must have gone down the ramp alive with their vehicles; so must the grooms and wagon drivers. Woolley thought they must have walked quietly

28

to their places at the funeral as some compelling custom of royal service or religious imperative required, and lain down after taking a drug. And then the pits were filled in. Only one tiny touch of human frailty disturbed the awesome discipline of the dead women— an untied silver ribbon, as if the owner had arrived late or been too nervous to fix it properly. But perhaps all the victims believed this would be only a temporary oblivion, after which they would awake and continue to serve their godlike king and queen in paradise.

Soon a discovery of a very different kind was made. The royal graves had been reached through layers of household rubbish, the accumulation of many centuries; but suddenly the nature of the earth below the domestic debris changed into clean fresh water clay without a particle of human remains or artifacts. This, however, was not the real surprise. The surprise was that after going down a further eight feet the explorers hit rubbish again as suddenly as the earlier layer had ceased. The layer of unadulterated clay could only be the result of some vast spread of water. In 1929, Woolley concluded these were traces of the Great Deluge of the Bible, and sent back to London an electrifying telegram: 'We have found the Flood.'

Flooding was, of course, common enough in the lower reaches of the two rivers, but this flood must have been colossal—covering perhaps an area 400 miles long and 100 miles wide. This is four-fifths of the size of England, or about the same size as Virginia or Ohio, but to the people of that age, it was their whole world. One further fact Woolley noticed. Though much of the pottery above and below the seam of pure clay was of the same kind, some that appeared below the seam did not reappear above it. Hence, he concluded, a whole community and its skills had been entirely wiped out in the catastrophe, which occurred some time between 3000 and 4000 BC. But was it the Bible Flood? Other excavations in Mesopotamia and elsewhere have revealed the occurrence of many floods at different times and at different levels, and archaeology has also unearthed other versions of the story of the Deluge than the well-known account in the Old Testament Book of Genesis.

There are wide variations in these accounts, but the similarities are more striking than the differences. The Book of Genesis records that when the ark was built 'Noah went in, and his sons, and his wife, and his sons' wives . . . and of everything that creepeth upon the earth, there went in two and two unto Noah into the ark, the male and the female . . .' And when the waters subsided and the ark

One of the Gilgamesh
tablets of the seventh
century BC, found at
Nineveh, in which
Utnapishtim describes
the Flood.

came to rest on Mount Ararat Noah opened the window of the ark
and sent out the raven, and then doves to see if dry land had re-
appeared. In an Assryian version of the Deluge in cuneiform on clay
tablets found at the site of Nineveh, 75 years before Woolley's excavations at Ur, a man named Utnapishtim built a vessel, and describes how 'All that I had I loaded, of the seed of all living things, I
brought into the ship my whole family and kinsfolk: the cattle of the
field, the beasts of the field, all craftsmen—I made them go up into it'.
Seven days later there was a lull in the downpour (Noah's storm
lasted forty days and the Flood 150 days) and the vessel grounded
on Mount Nisir, which lies in the Kurdistan range. Utnapishtim
sent out birds, but in a different order from Noah's—a dove first
and then a swallow—both fruitlessly, and finally a raven which found
a resting place and did not return. The most widely accepted in-
ference from the Mesopotamian discoveries is that there were a
number of floods in that period of history, but perhaps one was of
such devastating violence and range that it formed the basis of
several enduring and related sets of folklore.

In Mesopotamia the Sumerians built ziggurats. In the Assyrian-
Babylonian language ziggurat means 'to be high or raised up' and

so signifies a staged tower; these were not tombs for their kings but shrines to their gods. Every city had one and the great brickwork stump whose surface Taylor had scratched was the ziggurat of Ur, the main feature in a temple complex dedicated to the moon god Nannar. Today we can easily visualise what it must have been like, from a description of the ziggurat at Babylon written by the Greek historian of the fifth century BC, Herodotus. It was, he wrote:

'. . . a tower of solid masonry, a furlong square, upon which was raised a second tower, and on that a third and so on up to eight. The ascent is on the outside, by a path which winds round all the towers. When one is about half way up one finds a resting place and seats, where persons are wont to sit some time on their way to the summit. On the topmost tower there is a spacious temple, and inside the temple stands a couch of unusual size, richly adorned with a golden table by its side. There is no statue of any kind set up in the place, nor is the chamber occupied of nights by any one but a single native woman, who, as the Chaldeans, the priests of this god, affirm, is chosen for himself by the deity out of all the women of the land.'

The ziggurat at Ur, built about 2100 BC, would have been very similar in style, except that three separate staircases rising steeply in front and to either side of the facade gave access to the first of three terraces which Woolley guessed had once been planted with trees to provide shade.

But beyond the precincts of the ziggurat and the temple, what was Ur itself like—this city that the Bible says Terah left with his family to seek a better future for his people elsewhere?

Woolley's team laid bare the skeleton of a town. We can only guess at the homes of the poor: in a feudal society they would be small and of poor and perishable material. But we have a glimpse of their standard of living. Around the ziggurat were a number of buildings which were identified as tax-collecting depots, law courts, factories and various workshops. Business tablets and ledgers have been found which record receipts for tax payments, court judgments, and the names of women weavers of woollen cloth. We even know that as part of their wages they got food rations. Inscribed tablets now in the Iraq Museum in Baghdad record the distribution to them of about $5\frac{1}{2}$ pints of oil, 14 pint measures of fish, 15 pint measures of barley, and occasional quantities of dates. The tablets do not tell us how long such rations were supposed to last. Groups of

31

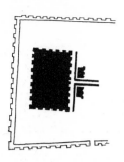

Reconstructed ground plan of the ziggurat at Ur.

weavers were also allotted portions of mutton.

By the year 2000 BC houses in the south of the town which had been built on the ruins of earlier ones and had later collapsed in their turn, had created an artificial hill, and its slopes were cut into terraces to provide foundation platforms for still more houses. Thus, at the time of Abraham, in the first half of the second millennium BC—that is, before 1500 BC—the houses of the wealthier citizens of Ur stood at various levels. They were built of mud bricks covered with plaster and whitewash. They had up to fourteen rooms built in two storeys around a central paved court which was open to the sky. The streets between these houses were narrow, twisting and unpaved. As protection against burglars the walls of the houses forming the sides of the streets had no windows. Mounting blocks showed that donkeys were used for riding and for carrying goods, and corners in the narrow lanes were rounded so that neither riders nor goods were jabbed on sharp edges.

The front door of the wealthier homes led into a small lobby with a drain in the middle where a visitor could wash. (Lice in hair and beard were a common affliction and the people used oil as well as water to combat the irritant.) From the lobby one passed to the central court, which was surrounded by perhaps half a dozen smallish rooms facing onto it. Some of these rooms would communicate with each other, and all would be accessible from the courtyard. Brick-built stairs ascended from one side of the courtyard to upper rooms and to a flat roof where the family could sit in the cool of the evening or sleep on summer nights. Behind the stairs was a lavatory with a terra cotta drain. On the ground floor were also a kitchen with a fireplace, a parlour, and in some houses a private chapel.

When, on top of these discoveries, Woolley's expedition found clay tablets copying hymns used in the temple and mathematical tablets which gave the formulae for extracting square and cube roots, they asked themselves whether Terah and Abraham had been much more sophisticated people than the Bible leads one to believe, or whether, if they were simple trekkers leading their people and their flocks to another country, as the Bible represents them, they could really have been citizens of this highly civilised city.

Excavations at Ur yielded no positive answer to the riddle of Abraham. But Woolley found intriguing evidence to support another famous Bible narrative. Ur was destroyed by the Babylonians in 1885 BC, and did not fully recover for three or four centuries, when another Babylonian warlord restored its temples. But afterwards

A pit excavated by Sir Leonard Woolley at Ur. The floor dates back to about 2900 BC, and the square opening at the foot leads into the 'Flood deposit'.

came another long period of neglect before the next great Babylonian builder, Nebuchadrezzar, undertook a vast reconstruction in the sixth-seventh century BC. Woolley's team traced reconstruction and repair of the temples of the moon god stretching over a period of seventeen centuries, from 2300 BC to 600 BC and found that Nebuchadrezzar had opened up the hitherto enclosed and secret sanctuary of the temple so that people could watch the priest making sacrifices at an open-air altar, and see through the sanctuary's open door behind him the image of the moon god. Now, the Bible says that Nebuchadrezzar made a great image and set it up in a public place and ordered everybody to fall down and worship it. This applied equally to the Jews who had been taken into captivity by Nebuchadrezzar, but three of them, Shadrach, Meshach and Abednego, faithful to their one invisible God, refused to obey. They chose instead to face death by burning, but miraculously survived the fiery furnace, and so converted the perplexed and frightened king. Woolley found that the layout of the temple ruins fitted the Bible story with striking accuracy.

The last king to build at Ur was Cyrus the Persian who died in 529 BC, and an inscribed brick of his is almost a repetition of the decree quoted by the Hebrew prophet Ezra allowing the Jews exiled in Babylonia to return and restore their Temple in Jerusalem. But after this Ur passed out of historical and political significance, though not mainly by the action or inaction of man. The river Euphrates had washed the western walls of Ur, and the city had always profited from the waterborne trade from the Persian Gulf and other towns along its course. But now the river began to veer away. Today it flows more than ten miles to the east of the ruins of Ur. Commerce carried by boats must have diminished progressively, and then ceased. The people moved away, the houses fell into disrepair, and the dust blew over it from the unwatered flatlands, undisturbed until Mr Taylor, vice-consul at Basra, came to probe it in 1854.

## BABYLON

Babylon has come down to us as the name of a place where pagan licence and barbaric splendour reached a peak. Its dried-up remains lie on the middle reaches of the Euphrates just north of the Iraqi market town of Hillah. It was once an undistinguished Akkadian market town itself, until it swelled into one of those city-states of the river-lands and a line of powerful semitic warlords made it their headquarters.

Sixth in this line was a king called Hammurabi. Scholars have dated him as early as 2123 BC and as late as 1700 BC, which is about contemporary with Abraham. He subdued both Sumer in the south and Akkadia, including Assyria, in the north, and he made Babylon the capital of a new territorial and commercial empire. But his successors lost this power, and for more than 1,000 years Babylonia was controlled by various other peoples, until Nebuchadrezzar (about 605 to 562 BC) made Babylon the centre of a vast system of fortifications. He built streets, canals, temples and palaces. He also commissioned the building of the fabled hanging gardens on a series of terraces, in order to assuage the homesickness of his Median wife, Amytis, for her native mountains. It was Hammurabi and Nebuchadrezzar, out of all the masters of Babylon, who had most impact on the history of the early Hebrew people and the Bible story.

Claudius James Rich, a brilliant young English linguist appointed the East India Company's representative in Baghdad in 1811, was the first European to investigate the ruins of Babylon, but French archaeologists can claim the real pioneering credit. In 1784 the Abbé J. de Beauchamp had found local peasants plundering the site for ready building material, and had rescued a few inscribed tablets which he sent back to Paris. German scholars began a more systematic exploration in 1899, but it was another Frenchman, Jacques de Morgan, who made the first great Babylonian discovery and brought Hammurabi's claim to fame out of the obliterating dust. This was not among the ruins of Babylon itself, however, but at Susa on the eastern edge of the Tigris valley.

In January 1902 his expedition dug up three lumps of black diorite stone which together formed a great slab about 42 feet square, covered back and front with 34 horizontal columns of cuneiform script. It was Hammurabi's Code of Laws, and had evidently been looted from Babylon in the days of its decline. Above the inscription is a *bas relief* of the king receiving the code from the sun god Shamash, just as, centuries later, Moses received God's laws for the Israelites on Mount Sinai. There are 248 laws, plus forty others that have been defaced at some time, and some of the laws have striking parallels with the laws of Moses as they are set out in the Books of Exodus and Deuteronomy. Here are some examples:

A model of the Ishtar Gate at Babylon.

*Hammurabi:* If a man has stolen ox, or sheep or ass, whether from the temple or the palace, he shall pay thirtyfold. If from a poor man, he shall render tenfold. If the thief cannot pay he shall be put to death.

*Moses:* If a man shall steal an ox, or a sheep, and kill it or sell it, he shall restore five oxen for an ox, and four sheep for a sheep . . . If he hath nothing, then he shall be sold for his theft.

*Hammurabi:* If a man has stolen the young son of a freeman he shall be put to death.

*Moses:* He that stealeth a man, and selleth him, or if he be found in his hand, he shall surely be put to death.

*Hammurabi:* If a man has put away his bride who has not borne him children he shall give her as much money as her bride-price, and shall pay her the marriage portion which she brought from her father's house, and shall put her away.

*Moses:* When a man hath taken a wife and married her, and it come to pass that she find no favour in his eyes . . . then let him write a bill of divorcement, and give it in her hand, and send her out of his house.

*Hammurabi:* If a man has caused the loss of an eye to a person of the upper class one shall cause his eye to be lost. If he has shattered his limb one shall shatter his limb.

*Moses:* If a man cause a blemish in his neighbour; as he hath

36

done so shall it be done to him; breach for breach, eye for eye, tooth for tooth . . .

These are the closest resemblances, and there are also great differences; but the Hammurabi stone shows that a code of laws quite as elaborate as that of Moses was in force in the lands from which Abraham came, many centuries before the time of Moses.

Archaeological exploration at Babylon itself has shown that in Hammurabi's time the city was destroyed by fire; and the remains found are almost entirely the work of Nebuchadrezzar. The most conspicuous of them were the double Gate of Ishtar, Great Mother of the Gods, which passed through the double wall of the main fortifications, and a processional street leading from the Gate to the main Temple of Marduk. The walls of this street were decorated with reliefs of hundreds of bulls and dragons, executed in colours and glazed bricks, and facing and menacing anyone who entered the Ishtar Gate. Nebuchadrezzar himself described the Gate: 'doorways of cedar covered with copper, threshold and hinges of bronze I fitted into its gates'. They opened into a complex of pink and blue and white temples, palaces and bazaars.

In 605 BC Nebuchadrezzar had inherited a revived Babylonian empire which his father had wrested from a declining Assyria. It was not an entirely docile empire, and in Palestine in 598 BC, King Jehoiakim of Judah plotted rebellion along with the kings of Tyre and Sidon, Ammon, Edom and Moab. To meet this threat Nebuchadrezzar marched on Jerusalem, aiming to cut the heart out of the revolt. Jehoiakim died before the Babylonian army reached the outskirts of his capital, but the Book of Kings tells us how Nebuchadrezzar deported the new king, Jehoiakim's eighteen-year-old son Jehoiachin, to Babylon, along with his mother and courtiers. Nebuchadrezzar's archives, found in the ruins of Babylon, are mostly concerned with his building exploits, but in 1903 a German expedition led by Professor Robert Koldewey, found tablets near the Ishtar Gate giving Nebuchadrezzar's own version of his punishment of Judah. These, however, lay unread for another thirty years in the cellars of a Berlin museum. Then in 1933, when Koldewey had been dead for eight years, another Assyriologist, E. F. Wiedner, was sorting out tablets in the museum cellar one day when he came across cuneiform inscriptions describing the deportation of King Jehoiachin. The account confirms the Bible story but is much more personal, with details showing a merciful side to Nebuchadrezzar which not unnaturally is omitted from the chronicles of the aggrieved people. For

Detail of brickwork on the Ishtar Gate

example, in order to show some respect for his prisoner's rank (and at the same time, no doubt, in order to keep a close eye on him) Nebuchadrezzar gave Jehoiachin and his entourage lodgings in his own palace, and the tablets in Berlin recorded the amount of food they were allowed from the royal pantries. Jehoiachin himself received barley and about three and a quarter gallons of sesame oil, probably representing a month's rations.

Full confirmation of the Bible narrative of the revolt in Judah did not come to light until 1955. Deciphering some other Babylonian cuneiform tablets in the British Museum, D. J. Wiseman found a report that Jerusalem was occupied by Nebuchadrezzar's troops on March 2, 597 BC, and it described how they 'took the king prisoner and appointed in his stead a king after their own heart'. This was the king's uncle, Zedekiah. But nine years later Zedekiah himself rebelled against the overlordship of Babylon and this time Nebuchadrezzar's vengeance was devastating. He wiped out Judah, and by the mass deportation of the people began the Babylonian Captivity. It lasted only seventy years because the days of Babylon itself were numbered.

In his 43-year reign until his death in 562 BC, Nebuchadrezzar brought his empire to a new peak of prosperity, but his successors were short-lived mediocrities. Belshazzar who, in the Bible, is named as the son of Nebuchadrezzar, but was more probably his grandson, acted as regent whilst his presumed father Nabonidus was away from his capital for twelve years campaigning against local rebellions in his realm. So, in effect, Belshazzar was the last real ruler of Babylon.

The riotous feast Belshazzar gave for a thousand of his nobles, their wives and his own womenfolk, is related in the Book of Daniel. The Greek historian Xenophon tells the same story: he fought in the Persian civil wars that followed the Persian conquest of Babylon by Cyrus in 538 BC, and probably heard it during his military service. Belshazzar had ordered up from the vaults the sacred vessels of gold and silver that Nebuchadrezzar had plundered from the Jewish Temple in Jerusalem, and all were drinking and mocking the God of the Jews (by praising their own idols of gold, silver, brass, iron, wood and stone) when a spectral hand appeared in the candlelight, writing mysterious words on the plaster wall. Belshazzar saw the hand and was terrified: the Bible says his knees knocked, and when his own soothsayers failed (or feared) to interpret the writing, his queen urged him to send for the Jewish prophet Daniel

Part of the full-sized reconstruction of the Ishtar Gate in the Vorderasiatische Museum, Berlin.

to explain the ghostly message.

Daniel came and declared that the writing on the wall meant that the end of the Babylonian kingdom was near and that it would be divided up between the Medes and Persians. And the Persians came. The Medes inhabited what is now western Iran and Soviet Azerbaijan. The Persian army led by Cyrus conquered the old capital of the Medes (modern Hamadan in Iran where the famous carpets are made), vanquished Assyria, and what is now Turkish Anatolia. When Cyrus marched on decadent Babylon it was ripe for surrender and gave in without a fight.

This was the end of Babylonian power; it became a mere satrapy of the new Persian empire. Bricks found at Ur bearing the name of Cyrus, record that 'the great gods have delivered all the lands into my hands'—a striking resemblance to the proclamation of Cyrus recorded in the Bible's Book of Ezra: 'The Lord God of Heaven hath given me all the kingdoms of the earth; and hath charged me to build him an house at Jerusalem.'

As we have seen, if he did not carry this out himself, Cyrus went out of his way to permit the Jews to return to their home for that purpose, and gave them back the sacred vessels that Nebuchadrezzar had looted from their Temple and Belshazzar's drinking party had defiled.

When Alexander the Great came on his conquering way in 330 BC, he found the great ziggurat of Babylon which Herodotus had described only a hundred years earlier, and which is thought to have been the one that figures in the Bible as the Tower of Babel, had been totally destroyed. Alexander passed on to India. On his way back, at the age of 33, he died of fever on June 13 323 BC, in the ruins of Nebuchadrezzar's Babylon.

## NINEVEH

Among the Assyrian clay tablets which have survived from about 2300 BC is one which reads:

'Sargon, the mighty king, King of Agade am I. My mother was a changeling, my father I knew not. My uncles loved the hills. My city is Azupiranu, on the banks of the Euphrates. My changeling mother conceived me, in secret she bore me. She set me in a basket of rushes and sealed the lid with pitch. She cast me into the river . . . Akki, the drawer of water, lifted me out as he dipped his ewer . . . took me as his son . . . reared me . . . appointed me his gardener. While I was a gardener, Ishtar (goddess of fertility) granted me her love . . .'

There is a striking similarity between the early autobiography of Sargon the Great of Akkad, and the Bible story of Moses, who became the leader of his people in Egypt. The Sargon inscription goes on to relate that through Ishtar's influence he became cup-bearer to the king of Kish (the ruins of which lie midway between the Tigris and Euphrates rivers) but eventually dethroned his master, took the sceptre himself, and founded the first Akkadian and semitic dynasty in Mesopotamia. His conquests went as far north as Asia Minor and so far south that he 'washed his weapons' in the Persian Gulf.

In about 1850 BC another Sargon became king, and then another, who founded the last Assyrian dynasty in 721. He was a soldier who seized the throne when his king died on a southern campaign while besieging Samaria. It was *this* Sargon's son, Sennacherib (704–681 BC), who fortified the city of Nineveh as his capital, surrounding an area of 1,800 acres (about three times the size of the City of London) with walls seven and a half miles long. Lying on the eastern side of the Tigris across from the modern city of Mosul, the line of the walls is traceable today in a series of mounds, with gaps where there used to be fifteen city gates. Inside the walls are two major mounds. The northern one is called Kuyunjik. The other is called Nebi Yunus, and the Bible says that the prophet Jonah went there at God's bidding to warn the wicked city that if it did not mend its ways it would be destroyed within forty days. Led by its king, according to the Book of Jonah, the people of Nineveh put on a great show of contrition, so that God relented—much to Jonah's disgruntlement.

Ancient Nineveh was first surveyed and mapped in modern times by Claudius Rich, but the first Englishman to excavate there was Henry Layard, a young lawyer who had been appointed an attaché at Constantinople. He had already created a sensation in 1847 by uncovering at Nimrud early Assyrian palaces and a magnificent black obelisk covered with an account of the military campaigns of King Shalmaneser III, a contemporary and enemy of Israel's King Ahab. The account was in cuneiform which at that time nobody in London could read. At Kuyunjik in Nineveh, Layard found the ruins of the main palace of Sennacherib. In these ruins were nearly two miles of wonderful sculptured reliefs, and—even more precious— part of a great national library. A second library compiled by his grandson, Ashurbanipal, in whose reign from 668 to 627 BC Assyria reached its highest point in wealth, art and learning was discovered in 1854.

Sennacherib was king of Nineveh when Hezekiah of Judah tried to break away from Assyrian control. Three books of the Bible— Kings, Chronicles, and Isaiah—record the curious course of Sennacherib's response to the revolt: for Sennacherib besieged Jerusalem and retreated from it, yet somehow obtained a capitulation (expressed in terms of tribute paid) from Hezekiah. A clay cylinder found at Nineveh records the campaign, but makes no mention of the retreat— not unnaturally, since Sennacherib had no interest in recording his failures.

The fullest account of Sennacherib's eight campaigns was found recorded on a large six-sided prism of the year 686 BC, uncovered

This hexagonal clay column describing his victorious campaigns was prepared for Sennacherib as a monument for a new palace at Nineveh in 689 BC. It includes an account of the siege of Hezekiah in Jerusalem.

at Nineveh; the third campaign reports operations against Judah:

'Then I besieged Hezekiah of Judah, who had not submitted to my yoke, and I captured forty-six of his strong cities and fortresses and innumerable small cities which were round about them, with the battering rams and the assault of engines and the attack of infantry and by mines and breaches . . . Himself (Hezekiah) like a caged bird I shut up within Jerusalem his royal city. I threw up mounds against him, and I took vengeance upon any man who came forth from this city . . . The fear of the majesty of my sovereignty overwhelmed Hezekiah, and the Urbi and his trusty warriors, whom he had brought into his royal city of Jerusalem to protect it, deserted. And he despatched after me his messenger to my royal city Nineveh to pay tribute and to make submission with 30 talents of gold, 800 talents of silver, precious stones, eye paint, ivory couches and thrones, hides and tusks, precious woods,

Sir Henry Layard's excavations at Nineveh. A drawing by S. C. Malan, 1852.

43

and divers objects, a heavy treasure, together with his daughters and the women of his palace and male and female musicians.'

The Bible confirms Hezekiah's humiliation and that he told Sennacherib, 'I have offended; return from me: that which thou puttest on me I shall bear. And the King of Assyria appointed unto Hezekiah, King of Judah, 300 talents of silver and 30 talents of gold. And Hezekiah gave him all the silver that was found in the house of the Lord, and in the treasures of the king's house . . .' And since Sennacherib's army withdrew without subduing Jerusalem, it looks as if Hezekiah bought him off. In a second campaign however, there is speculation that Hezekiah defied Sennacherib, and was saved only by a mysterious catastrophe that struck the Assyrian troops. The Bible says, 'And it came to pass that night that the angel of the Lord went out, and smote in the camp of the Assyrians an hundred four-score and five thousand. And when they arose early in the morning, behold, they were all dead corpses. So Sennacherib, king of Assyria, departed, and went and returned, and dwelt at Nineveh.'

A startling explanation has been offered by the Greek historian Herodotus. When Hezekiah revolted, Egypt seems to have promised support, so Sennacherib was really campaigning against Egypt. And Herodotus reports that an Egyptian priest told him that as the Assyrians approached the Egyptian frontier 'An army of field mice swarmed over their opponents in the night . . . gnawed through their quivers and their bows, and the handles of their shields, so that on the following day they fled without their arms and a great number of them fell. Hence, this king (of Egypt) still stands in Hephaestus's temple with a mouse in his hand, and with the inscription, "Look on me and live in safety".'

For people in Bible times the mouse had the same terror as the rat; it was a symbol of plague. In 1938, on the edge of the city of Lachish which Sennacherib also besieged in the same campaign, James L. Starkey, a British archaeologist, found a mass grave of 2,000 skeletons. If it was not the mice that decimated Sennacherib's army, it looks as if it were hit by some disabling epidemic.

The Bible reports that when Sennacherib returned home he was assassinated by his sons, Adrammelech and Sharezer, who then fled to Armenia, so that a third son, Esarhaddon, inherited the throne of Assyria. Tablets found in Nineveh confirm the story and are more precise: they say the murder occurred in January 681 BC, in the twenty-third year of the king's reign. Other inscriptions written at the dictation of Esarhaddon give a clue to the patricidal plot.

Lion hunt relief from Ashurbanipal's palace at Nineveh.

'Disloyal thoughts inspired my brothers . . . They rebelled. In order to use royal power they killed Sennacherib . . .' Esarhaddon goes on to say, 'I ascended my father's throne with joy. The south wind was blowing . . . whose breezes are propitious for royal authority . . . I am Esarhaddon, king of the world . . .'

Esarhaddon's younger son, Ashurbanipal, the grandson of Sennacherib, succeeded to the throne in 668 BC. He was well-trained in warfare and manly sports, but he was also a scholar. He learned to read and write cuneiform, and under his enlightened rule Assyria enjoyed a golden age of learning in the seventh century BC. Ashurbanipal was the first great private collector of books known to history. He sent scribes to all the towns which then possessed 'books' (meaning inscribed clay tablets)—Asshur, Babylon, Cuthan, Nippur, Akkad, Erech—and copied some of them himself when they reached Nineveh. About 25,000 tablets from his library were brought to the British Museum. They range in size from less than one inch square to fifteen inches by eight and a half, and consist of letters, contracts, sales, loans, dictionaries, grammars, prayers, oracles, astrology, history, geography, law and literature.

Among all these riches the most interesting for those searching for Bible links was one group of tablets identified in the British Museum by a young man named George Smith. He had taught himself to read cuneiform, and in 1870 he found an allusion to the Assyrian version of the Creation. Then, in 1872, he discovered tablets containing the Assyrian version of the Flood. On the strength of these discoveries Smith went out to Mesopotamia and there he found still more tablets. The story of the Creation was written on

45

seven of them. Let us see how it compares with the Bible version. The Book of Genesis begins, 'In the beginning God created the heaven and the earth. And the earth was waste and void . . .' The tablets said, 'When the heavens were yet unnamed and the name of the earth beneath had not been recorded,' there was chaos.

Then, according to the tablets, gods were produced and divided between good and evil. Marduk was chosen champion against the evil gods, and out of the body of his defeated enemy Tiamat, he created heaven and earth, afterwards setting the stars in their courses, fixing the period of a year, and nominating the moon god to rule the night. It reads like a descant on the Bible narrative. Then Marduk said to another god named Ea, 'I will solidify blood, I will form bone; I will set up man.' The Genesis version of how man first arrived on earth is as follows: 'And the Lord God formed man of the dust of the ground, and breathed into his nostrils the breath of life; and man became a living soul.'

Ashurbanipal set out on various now forgotten military campaigns. His successes as a warrior-king were insignificant compared with his cultural achievements. But his two sons who succeeded him, one after the other, had none of their father's flair for learning or warfare, and within eighteen years of Ashurbanipal's death his sons had squandered their inheritance and brought Assyria to its nadir. In 612 BC Scythians and Medes besieged Nineveh and in August of that year they took it, looted its temples and the homes of the rich, and then destroyed it. A vague but poignant chronicle indicates that Ashurbanipal's second son, Sinsharishkur, died in the flames of the burning palace. With him died Assyria.

# 3

# The Walls of Jericho

Jericho is the oldest known site of successive human settlement in the world. Archaeologists have shown that nearly 7,000 years ago there were houses in Jericho with polished floors. These floors met the walls in an upward curve so that no dust could collect where walls and floor met—a refinement that modern house-builders have forgotten.

One way of trying to grasp the great age of Jericho is to say that it had become a ruin of layer upon layer of lost cities—and a new town had risen beside it—by the time Jesus came by and spent the night in the house of the rich tax-gatherer Zacchaeus, who was so small, St Luke tells us, that he had to climb into a sycamore tree to see Jesus over the heads of the excited crowd. But ancient Jericho has no recorded history like other famous places in the world, and were it not that the Bible makes it the scene of one of the most dramatic episodes of the Old Testament it might never have been remembered at all.

Jericho owed its earliest settlement and its immense span of life to a spring whose waters travel from beneath the Judean hills and emerge at the rate of 6,000 gallons an hour. This spring would make it a notable place for rest and refuge among the earliest nomads, for the waters turn Jericho into a garden in the middle of the desert, a great oasis where date palms fount their golden fruit in a never-ending summer. Jericho lies 800 feet below sea level on the western side of the lower Jordan valley and the heat cupped in this dent in the earth sometimes rises to 130 degrees in the shade. But there is no winter cold. Bananas ripen in December.

The spring flows out of the western flank of a hill about a mile

Details of carved bone inlay on a Bronze Age box, Jericho

47

OPPOSITE
*Above* Gaming board
with two sets of
playing pieces found
at Ur. Shell, lapis
lazuli, bone and
coloured paste were
used in the inlay work,
with bitumen as an
adhesive.
*Below* One side of
the so-called 'Standard
of Ur', a four-sided
wooden structure
decorated in a mosaic
of shell, red limestone
and lapis lazuli inlaid
in bitumen. The king
banquets among his
nobles to the sound
of music, while
tributaries bring cattle,
asses and other gifts.

and a half north of the modern town, and close by the spring is a great mound, or tell. A tell is a man-made hill of settlements, each built on the ruins of the one before. This tell is ancient Jericho.

Jericho comes into the Bible story at a crucial point in the history of the Jews. We have seen how the Hebrew tribes were led by the Patriarchs in a series of journeys that brought them to bondage in Egypt. Abraham and his caravan must have carried with them the folk memories of life in Mesopotamia, yet when they escaped from Egypt under the leadership of Moses, they travelled with something quite new: a religious conception which owed nothing to legions of Mesopotamian gods, and which was to distinguish them from all other ancient people. This was the conception that there was only one god. And since it was because of God's intervention that the fleeing Hebrews survived, they considered themselves to be his favoured folk: 'Henceforth I am your God and you are my people.' This was the Covenant between them, and the Ark (which the Israelites afterwards carried with them) was the visible symbol of the bond.

Until recent times the story of the Exodus from Egypt was accepted as the one and only origin of the Israelites, but in the light of modern research and archaeology it is now generally accepted that the Bible story is an over-simplification: that in fact those who followed Moses to the frontiers of the Promised Land represented only one section of migrating Hebrews. It is now believed that several groups penetrated Canaan over a period of time, rather than in one campaign of conquest, and that only later did these groups come together to form a union as Israelites. It is further argued that the separate experiences of these groups were later woven together into a narrative of Hebrew wandering. Yet the distinction of the Hebrews remained—their religious belief in a single, all-powerful and sufficient God of whom they, among all mankind, had become the special care and concern.

Moses himself did not live long enough to take his people into the Promised Land. The man entrusted with the task of bringing the Exodus to its preordained conclusion was Joshua.

Nobody knows for certain when Joshua lived. Some scholars have decided it was about 1400 BC and some thought—and still think—it was nearer 1230 BC. In the Bible story he was instructed to lead the Israelites into the Promised Land after they had wandered in the wilderness for forty years. They approached Canaan from the east out of Moab, Joshua first sending out spies to 'view the land,

Carved Bronze Age
amethyst scarab seal,
Jericho

48

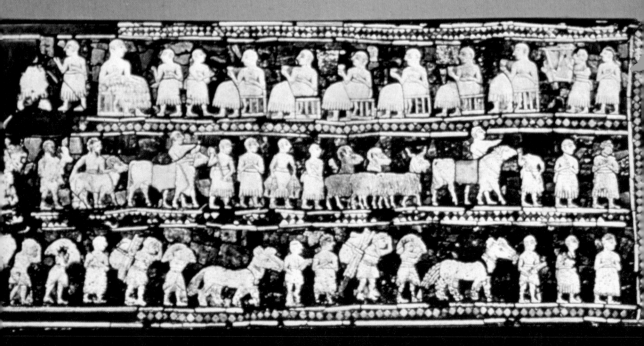

even Jericho'. Joshua himself must have looked across the Jordan river and seen how the barren sand they were leaving was here darkened with clumps of tamarisk trees; five miles beyond the farther bank of the river he must have seen brilliant green fields watered by the spring of Jericho.

The Israelites camped on the River Jordan's eastern bank for three days, during which Joshua went among his people reminding them of the pledge that God would not fail them. The Ark of the Covenant would be borne before them: the sacred symbol of their God would guarantee victory.

When the priests, carrying the Ark, stepped out off the banks of the river, the waters, say the Bible, 'stood and rose up upon an heap' upstream, so that the Israelites were able to cross the emptied bed of Jordan. Looking out over their walls the Jerichoans saw Joshua's host approaching, and closed the city gates. 'Now Jericho was straitly shut up because of the Children of Israel: none went out, and none came in.' It must have looked like the beginning of a long and formidable siege.

Joshua decided first to intimidate the inhabitants. We would now call this device psychological warfare. He ordered his troops, led by priests blowing rams' horn trumpets, to march round the city once a day for six days. At dawn on the seventh day he brought his tactics to a climax by marching round the city seven times. As they came round the seventh time, trumpets blaring, Joshua commanded all his people to shout, and as they did so, the walls of Jericho 'fell down flat, so that the people went up into the city, every man straight before him, and they took the city'. Joshua then 'burnt the city with fire', destroyed all that was in it, and put a curse on any man who should rebuild on the ruins of his conquest.

The Bible tells us nothing more about the city for hundreds of years, until the reign of Ahab, King of Israel from 874 to 853 BC. 'In his days,' says the Old Testament, 'did Hiel the Bethelite build Jericho.' The prophets Elijah and Elisha went to the new Jericho, and once, when drought hit the land, Elisha cast salt into the waters of the spring and restored their sweetness. The spring has since been called Elisha's Fountain.

Nearly three hundred years later, in 587 BC, Nebuchadrezzar, King of Babylon, conquered Judah, and when Judah's King Zedekiah saw the mighty Babylonian army surrounding Jerusalem, he fled 'to the plains of Jericho'. The Babylonians destroyed most of the towns in the region, and Jericho was abandoned. Palestine itself became a

The site of ancient Jericho, lying between the modern city and the huts used by Palestine refugees.

49

The overlapping impression of two circular rush mats still shows on the floor of a house in Jericho built nearly 7,000 years ago.

battleground of rival powers for hundreds of years. When the Romans arrived, their vassal Herod built a winter palace south-west of the old town of Jericho, and the Egyptian queen Cleopatra came to stay with him. Fifty years later the Jewish historian Josephus records how 'palm trees, both many in number and excellent in kind' caught the covetous eyes of Cleopatra, and so did the balsam, much sought after as a drug in those days and obtained from trees in Jericho. Her avarice did not abate when she returned home, because Josephus goes on to say that Herod eventually 'farmed to her parts of Arabia and those revenues that came to her from the region about Jericho'. Herod hated doing this but he had no choice. He even had a notion to murder Cleopatra during her visit, but despite his experience as an assassin (he strangled two of his own sons and had a third beheaded) he was too afraid of Cleopatra's powerful lover Antony and of Rome to carry it out.

Jericho had become a Roman winter resort when Jesus crossed the Jordan, probably by the same fording place that Joshua had used, and lodged with Zacchaeus.

As their empire weakened the Romans retreated from the Jordan valley, and Jericho once more lapsed into neglect. In 325 AD it had a brief revival as a pleasant place where the wealthier Jerusalem people spent the cold months of the year, and some seven hundred years later, at the time of the Crusades, a third Jericho arose about a mile east of the Old Testament site. But when the Crusaders left, this also declined, to revive only in our own times as part of the modern kingdom of Jordan. All that has survived without any interruption is the spring that helped to identify the grey hump of Tell es-Sultan beside it as the remains of the ancient city it once served.

To archaeologists the layers of earth and stone in such a mound are like the pages of a thick history book. They open such books by digging down through the last pages to the first. The first person to try to do this at Jericho was a Briton named Captain Charles Warren in 1867. But when he had dug a deep hole in the tell, it was as if he had bored right through the book without being able to open the pages, and he was incapable of reading the edges.

An Austro-German expedition between 1907 and 1909 was the first to find ancient fortified walls, but at this time the dating of pottery remains was undeveloped, and the expedition arrived at what are now considered to be faulty conclusions. Ancient pottery could be far more accurately identified and dated by the time Professor John Garstang of Liverpool University worked at the site between 1930 and 1936. He also dug deeper than the Germans had done and made what were then sensational discoveries going back to the late Stone Age—some 6,000 years ago.

The first defences he found he dated at about 3000 BC, and he called this the First City of Jericho. Garstang measured this 'city' out at no more than 250 yards long, consisting of houses huddled along walls of mud-slab bricks, separated by a narrow street from a double row of houses in the middle. He found farming tackle—sickle blades, silos, grain bins; the remains of food—millet, barley, lentils; fragments of cloth and grapeskins—indicating that the Jerichoans knew how to weave and how to make wine. But he found no weapons, from which it might be assumed that this was a time when no enemy threatened the desert settlement.

He dated a Second City from 2500 to 2000 BC, with new walls higher up the mound ten feet thick and made of yellow bricks. Signs of three-storey houses showed that the population was growing. A screen wall a little way down the slope perhaps showed that the fear of enemies was growing, too.

A Third City, dated by Garstang at 1900 to 1500 BC, showed a new population building a defensive stone bank 21 feet high and entirely enclosing a city area twice the size of the older one. Some of

the stones in this defensive wall weighed more than a ton; the inhabitants were evidently aware of possible attack by battering rams. The Hyksos, a semitic people, appeared in Canaan about 1750 BC bringing with them a new style of defensive rampart and a new weapon of war—the horse-drawn chariot. They may well have been the new lords of Jericho, now nine acres in extent, and whose walls enclosed the entire water supply. In the heart of the city, on the most elevated spot, the explorers found remains of a palace surrounded by store rooms, offices and stables, which led to the theory that Jericho was developed as an advance base and commissariat for Hyksos invasion and conquest of Egypt.

In about 1600 BC the Egyptians counter-attacked and drove the Hyksos back to the borders of Syria. Canaan thus became a battleground and Professor Garstang, finding traces that the palace and houses had been burned, concluded that Jericho was destroyed in this period.

When it rose again its defences enclosed a diminished town at the brink of the hill top. There were still no written records to be found. Having dug a deep trench, the expedition team found and washed 150,000 fragments of pottery, but so much of this was new to archaeology that it gave poor clues about the people of Jericho. What Garstang was looking for, of course, and in the end believed he had found, was what all archaeologists most wanted to find at Jericho— the walls that Joshua was said to have destroyed; for then he would not only have certified a layer of Jericho's history as a town, but would have corroborated scientifically the Old Testament stories.

In the Book of Kings it is written that 'in the four hundred and eightieth year after the children of Israel were come out of the land of Egypt, in the fourth year of Solomon's reign over Israel . . . he began to build the house of the Lord.' Relying on other sources that the fourth year of Solomon's kingship was 967 BC, and subtracting the forty years the Israelites spent in the wilderness after leaving Egypt, Professor Garstang calculated that the destruction of Jericho by Joshua must have been about 1407 BC. And he saw that this coincided with the period that he assigned to his Fourth City walls. The Bible says that Joshua finished off his siege by burning the city, and at this level Professor Garstang found traces of a great fire, compact masses of blackened bricks, cracked stones, and charred wood and ashes. So the Bible story seemed to have been dramatically confirmed.

If we feel inclined to discount miracles, it left only two questions

Successive cities of Jericho; a portion of town wall built on top of an earlier one.

The expedition led by Dr Kathleen Kenyon begins excavation at the earliest inhabited levels, at the base of Professor Garstang's trench. The top figures stand at the Jericho street level of about 2300 BC

about the taking of Jericho unanswered: why did the waters of the River Jordan pile up to allow the Israelites to cross over so conveniently, and what really made the walls of Jericho fall when the besieging army of Joshua shouted?

First, let us take the drying up of part of the river. The Jordan *could* have been blocked by a sudden landslide. On the night of December 7 1267 AD, for instance, a huge mound on the western bank collapsed into the river and dammed it so that the Jordan ceased to flow along its normal course for sixteen hours. There was another landslide in 1906, and a third in 1927 when no water flowed down the river bed below it for 21 hours.

And the fall of the walls? Professor Garstang believed that it could only be the result of an earthquake. Jericho lies in an earthquake zone that runs across Asia. But could earthquake and landslide have happened in roughly the same week? It is quite possible. But could both have occurred exactly at the times chosen by the Israelites to cross the Jordan and attack the first city in the Promised Land? To that question one can answer only that history is rich in startling coincidences.

The conclusions reached by Garstang have not all remained unchallenged. Another expedition began work at ancient Jericho in 1952 under Dr Kathleen Kenyon, Director of the British School of Archaeology in Jerusalem. Twelve years earlier a revolutionary method of dating remote artifacts had emerged as a by-product of atomic research. Mildly radioactive carbon (carbon with an atomic weight of 14) is contained in all organisms, but when an organism dies it stops taking in carbon from the atmosphere, and from then C14 diminishes at a known rate. Its half-life is about 5,568 years. This is halved again in the next 5,568 years, and so on. The time that has elapsed since the death of an organism can thus be calculated. Until this discovery was made the dating of finds in periods before history was set down in writing was based on the relative positions of artifacts—pottery, for example—dug out of the earth. Dr Kenyon had this new scientific instrument of carbon analysis at her command.

Digging at five different places on the ten-acre site, her team was able to trace human habitation back to the eighth millennium BC. Fifty feet down they came to bedrock and the roots of crude walls, not of houses or fortifications, but perhaps a shelter built by hunters of the Mesolithic Age because the never-failing spring was close by. They were far older than those Garstang had designated as the First City walls. A radio-carbon test gave a date around 7,800 BC, and although modern research has questioned the absolute accuracy of radio-carbon estimates, no settled habitation by man so far back in time had been found anywhere else on earth. And at this level civilised life began, because the next upward layer of earth showed that the descendants of the hunters built upon the first ruins which had been destroyed by fire, and it is on this evidence that Jericho is claimed to be the oldest town in the world.

Layer by layer the slow development of this civilisation could be read, first in the signs of man beginning to cultivate plants for food

In a Bronze Age tomb the skeleton of a man lies with weapons beside him and food for his journey into the next world.

OPPOSITE The finest
of the plastered and
painted skulls found
at Jericho.

instead of relying on wild growth, and harvesting crops with flint and bone implements. The first vessels found were scooped out of stone; after 3,000 years these were replaced with pottery. Next, man discovered the use of metal, and copper tools appeared. Ceramics were also produced. The remains of houses emerged in different styles of mud brick, and burnished floors of coloured plaster. Graves told their own story, too. People were buried with provisions to eat on their supposed journey to the next world: joints of mutton, a sheep's head, raisins, water pots with dipping cups. In the tomb of one woman lay a wooden bowl carved like a pomegranate and put in a basket along with fine wooden combs, a necklace of carnelians, a perfume bottle, and an amethyst charm. Beside male skeletons lay weapons for defence against whatever terrors might haunt travel beyond the grave. Heads were found severed from their bodies and covered with plaster to perpetuate their features when the flesh had decayed—some with cowrie shells stuck in to represent only half-closed eyes. Some plastered faces had been painted—the work of mankind's first portrait artists.

All this, however, was discovered in layers of Jericho much earlier than Biblical times. The excavators found that over one period of a thousand years seventeen successive town walls had been built to defend the city. The earliest had been destroyed by fire and so had the seventeenth; and all of them were earlier than the presumed dates of Joshua's assault. Where, then, were the fortifications that fell down flat at the trumpet blast?

Professor Garstang had taken his dating of the assault from the Bible account of the time that elapsed between the Exodus from Egypt and the known date of Solomon's reign, and so arrived at 1407 BC. But there is no scholarly agreement on the date when the Israelites left Egypt, and the walls designated by Professor Garstang as those destroyed at the time of Joshua's invasion of Canaan were reinterpreted by Dr Kenyon as belonging to the Early Bronze Age, which in the Middle East ended about 2100 BC. There had been a further destruction of Jericho soon after 1600 BC when the Egyptians drove out the Hyksos people. Dr Kenyon's work team found that on the eastern slopes of this town were closely-built houses through which ran two steep streets not unlike the narrow streets of old Jerusalem today, in parts made easier for pedestrians and animals by a series of wide and shallow cobbled steps. Houses opened directly onto the streets, and there were shops in which were found huge jars still holding the remains of grain.

Over the top of this demolished town the excavators came upon a thick seam of earth streaked with black, brown, white and pink ash, and they concluded that seasonal rains over a long period—perhaps nearly two hundred years—had washed this down from burned buildings higher up the sloping sides of Jericho. The process of decay had been halted when a new town was built on top of the wash in about 1400 BC. It is possible that city walls of the Middle Bronze Age, which lasted from 2100 BC to about 1580 BC, were still in use in Joshua's time; but of town walls built in the late Bronze Age—that is, from about 1580 BC to 1200 BC, within which period the attack by the Israelites under Joshua must fall by any dating—no identifiable trace did the Kenyon expedition find. In other words, though the walls that collapsed under Joshua's assault may have been uncovered, their disintegrated remains are now inextricably mixed with the debris of centuries.

The excavations did, however, throw up at the relevant earth layer one thing to be a seed of romantic speculation. It was a small portion of a building thought to have been part of a Canaanite kitchen. Beside the remains of an oven lay a small jug, as if hastily discarded. Was it dropped there by a frightened woman who fled her house at the first sign of an earth tremor—or at the alarming sound of trumpets and a great shout? Jericho has yielded up a story of man stretching back almost 10,000 years, but it holds back an answer to this Bible riddle. It seems unlikely now that an undisputable answer will ever be found.

# 4

# Jerusalem the Golden

In church on Sundays my grandfather sang his favourite hymn, 'Jerusalem the Golden' as if he were home-sick for his native town. But he never saw Jerusalem. He was a Yorkshire farmer without a drop of Jewish blood and he never travelled farther from home than London. Other Englishmen have shown the same passionate concern. Richard I of England—Richard the Lion Heart—who came to the throne in 1157, ruled in London, but cared more about going on a Crusade to try to capture Jerusalem for Christendom. A Muslim traveller in the tenth century wrote of Jerusalem how 'people find themselves drawn here . . . as if by some irresistible force,' and in the twelfth century another traveller, Benjamin of Tudela, remarked that its population was composed of 'people of all tongues'. Mark Twain was enraptured to see Jerusalem in 1867 'perched on its eternal hills, white, domed and solid', gleaming in the sun, and when he reached it he was surprised to find that it was no bigger than an American village.

Why has a far-off eastern city been such an enduring magnet for the western world? Why, indeed, did it ever become such an important city to the eastern world? It has no obvious advantages to be coveted by conquerors or commerce. It has no river; the sea is 34 miles away; it guards no strategic mountain pass; it stands on no main trade route. But it sits like a crown on the crest of the Judean hills and it has rare beauty. Its newest houses are built of pale yellow and rose-tinted stone that makes them look like small fortresses; and its huddled, ancient quarter glows like a honeycomb in the sunlit air. And it has more than beauty: it is an earthly focal point for three of the world's great religions. Jerusalem is holy to the Jews because it was David's capital and the home of their shrine to God. It is holy to Christians because Jesus preached and was crucified there. And it is a holy place to Muslims because they believe it was from the heart of Jerusalem that their prophet Mohammed climbed up a ladder to Heaven.

Jerusalem is about 3,800 years old—much older than the first Bible mention of it. Modern archaeologists are still trying to piece together its history from the jumbled remains of walls and streets that they have uncovered. But the first written record so far known was discovered in Egypt. In the first half of the second millennium BC the Egyptians practised a curious custom of inscribing the names of their enemies on jars and statuettes, and then ceremonially breaking them, hopefully believing that in so doing they struck a mortal blow at their enemies. These are the so-called execration texts, and in their remains has been found the first known mention of Jerusalem.

In 1887 an Egyptian peasant woman in El Amarna, near the Nile, found some clay tablets inscribed with strange writing. El Amarna had been the capital of the famous Pharaoh Akhenaten, and four years after the peasant woman's find, archaeologists began to excavate there. They found 377 of these clay tablets which turned out to be a whole royal archive of letters written to the Egyptian court by subject kings between the years 1390 BC and 1360 BC, when petty kings in Canaan were vassals of Egypt. One of these letters was from the man who governed 'Urusalim' and called himself Abdu-Heba. His was a frantic appeal for Egyptian help against local raiders. He accused especially Milkilu of Gezer, and Shuwardata of Hebron, towns only a few miles away. No response from the Pharaoh Akhenaten has been found.

Akhenaten showed little interest in the squabbles of local barons in his loose-held colonial empire, and there was an additional reason for his ignoring Abdu-Heba's cry for help: among the Amarna tablets was one written by Shuwardata of Hebron making exactly the same accusations of raiding against Abdu-Heba of Jerusalem as Abdu-Heba had made against him.

Canaan was reached by the Israelites shortly after this time, and Jerusalem may have been one of the walled cities that daunted them when Moses first sent out tribal scouts—including Joshua—to spy out the Promised Land. After capturing Jericho, Joshua made no attempt to tackle Jerusalem, which was then held by a people called the Jebusites. The Jebusites were still in possession 250 years later when David succeeded Saul as leader of the Hebrew tribes. He

The Pool of Siloam today. Into it still flow the waters of the Gihon spring through the Siloam Tunnel cut by Hezekiah's engineers.

shattered the Philistines and extended the power of the united tribes from Dan north of Galilee to Beersheba in the south. Jebusite Jerusalem lay about midway between these limits, and so, to make his kingdom secure, David, now 37 years of age, brought his army up the Judean hills and laid siege to it.

It was not like the Jerusalem we know today, but a modest little town built on a spur of hill south of the later expanded city of Solomon's day and south of the modern city. But it was strongly sited, with valleys on three sides and formidable walls. The Jebusites paraded on the ramparts their blind and crippled citizens as if to signal their scorn of David's threat. But the defences had a weakness. The source of the city's main water supply, called the Spring of Gihon in the Old Testament and known later to Christians as the Virgin's Fountain because of a legend that Mary washed Christ's napkins in its waters, lay deep in the eastern Kidron valley and outside the city walls. In time of siege any water-carriers venturing out of the city would be easy victims for an enemy.

In 1867, when the British explorer, Captain Charles Warren, visited the spring he saw the tunnel from which the water emerged and found a cavity in the roof. Warren had been an Alpine climber. Using ropes and a ladder he got up into this cavity and found it was

61

the bottom of a shaft that led up through the rock and into the city. The Book of Samuel reports that David announced to his soldiers that 'whosoever getteth up the gutter and smiteth the Jebusites and the lame and the blind . . . he shall be chief and captain,' and, as the story is continued in the Book of Chronicles, 'Joab, the son of Zeruiah, went up first and was chief.'

The commonest interpretation of this account is that David knew of the spring and its secret shaft—similar ancient springs and shafts have since been found elsewhere in Palestine—and that Joab led a picked commando unit into the tunnel, and then, climbing the shaft, breached the city's defences. But this explanation presented some difficulties. The shaft was narrow and in places vertical. Would not enemies emerging from it in Jerusalem be easily killed one by one?

Pondering this problem, the late Professor E. L. Sukenik, of the Hebrew University in Jerusalem, suggested that the Hebrew word *zinnor* be translated not as 'gutter' but as a weapon like a trident which is known to have been in use in David's time. The Hebrew letter for 'and' is W, and W is also the Hebrew suffix for 'his'. By moving the letter W back one space in the Hebrew Biblical text and reading it as the suffix of zinnor rather than a prefix for the succeeding word, there would emerge the phrase 'whosoever . . . smiteth . . . the lame and the blind with his trident . . .' The New English Bible now translates the word neither as gutter nor as trident, but as 'grappling iron'. These are, however, matters of philology, not archaeology. One speculative explanation could accommodate all three: perhaps David had a secret agent, a Jebusite traitor, in Jerusalem, and made use of him to help Joab's commando unit up the shaft with ropes just as Joshua had used a harlot as an agent to help his spies up the walls of Jericho.

The Bible narrative posed one further baffling problem. It was the Jewish historian, Josephus Flavius, a thousand years after David's capture of Jerusalem, who suggested that the Jebusites put the lame and the blind on the walls as a gesture of contempt—as if to say to David, 'Your threat is too ridiculous to make it necessary to summon the regular garrison to action stations.' But what stood at their gates was a formidable army, led by a victorious commander. Wasn't this too serious for such a gesture? Even more puzzling, if manning the battlements with invalids was a joke by the Jebusites, why should David's response be to offer the greatest prize—promotion to what must have been the rank of Chief of Staff—to the officer bold enough to strike the first blow?

Professor Yigael Yadin of Israel has offered a solution for the riddle. Ancient writing found in Turkey has revealed that the fear of disease was so great that it was used to intimidate troops whose loyalty to their warlord was doubtful. They were made to swear oaths in front of blind and deaf people, with the threat that if they failed in their fealty they would become similarly inflicted. If the dread of infection was being exploited by the Jebusites, then their action, far from being a gesture of derision, was more likely a last desperate throw—the only thing they could think of that might daunt David's assault troops. Whatever the explanation, David captured Jerusalem and made it his capital.

David brought the Ark of the Covenant into his new capital to give it a permanent home. It signified the end of the wandering of the Jewish tribes, and made Jerusalem holy as well as royal. For a place to house the Ark David bought for fifty silver shekels the breezy threshing floor of a Jebusite called Araunah, north of the city. He ordered building materials—stone, iron and cedar wood from Lebanon—and set aside cash to pay for it. But then he became convinced that his own hands were too stained with the blood of warfare to be the builder of God's pure sanctuary, so he willed the obligation to his favoured son Solomon, and until David died the Ark stayed in a tent.

David's Jerusalem was smaller than most English villages—barely half a mile from north to south and not much more than 200 yards wide. But Solomon, like many a rough pioneer's son, cultivated the richer settled life his father's conquest had made possible. He nursed his father's alliance with Phoenician Tyre (which is modern Sur in Lebanon), married one of the Egyptian Pharaoh's daughters, and built Israel into a great trading nation. Jerusalem was the heart of it. Solomon extended the city northward, more than doubling its walled area, and four years after he became king he began to build the House of the Lord on Araunah's threshing floor. It seems to have been a tall narrow building, 110 feet long and 48 wide, three storeys high, dimly lighted by slit windows, and with chambers for priestly use built up against the outer walls. It rose in reverent silence: stone was dressed before it was brought to the site so that no noise of masons' tools would be heard. The sanctuary was floored in pine, the walls and ceilings panelled in cedar, carved with fruit and flowers and then covered with gold leaf; so was an altar and two huge carved cherubim, the outer tips of whose combined wingspread reached from wall to wall. The doors, made out of beautiful lemon-

Ivory 'cherub' dis-
covered in Samaria.
Said to be similar to
those placed in the
Holy of Holies in
Solomon's Temple

and-brown-streaked olive wood, swung on golden hinges; the sanctuary furnishings were covered with gold—standard lamps, candle extinguishers, basins, knives, bowls and incense boats.

Hereditary priests, whose families still survive under the name of Cohen, conducted services; rabbis lectured in the outer courtyard. Solomon's palace and other royal apartments with their own court-yards occupied terraces below the Temple and took thirteen years to complete. In them were separate private quarters for Solomon's Egyptian wife, a throne room, and the 'house of the forest of Lebanon' —perhaps Solomon's law court and probably so called because its cedar beams rested on 45 cedar pillars. Hiram of Tyre came at Solomon's bidding to superintend extravagant ornamental metal-work, and made such things as bronze pillars 27 feet high, carved with two hundred pomegranates on each capital.

Such splendour cost a great deal of money. Solomon taxed the twelve provinces of his kingdom to foot the bill, and it may well be that the resentment this aroused was one of the factors leading to the break-up of his kingdom when he died in 930 BC. The northern tribes defected and Jerusalem became the capital only of the southern part of Canaan called Judah. It was held by the Jews for the next four hundred years or so, but not without difficulty and challenge. The most spectacular threat that we know of came in 701 BC when the famous prophet Isaiah was the people's spiritual adviser and Hezekiah was their king. Down from Assyria in the north came an invading army led by Sennacherib carrying all before it until it came in sight of Jerusalem. Hezekiah hastily made good the fortress walls where they had fallen into disrepair, worked the armourers night and day to make spears and shields, and walked the streets to en-courage his garrison and citizens. But he knew it would all be in vain if Sennacherib cut off Jerusalem's water supply. At the same time a besieging army would be in difficulties if *its* water supply were cut off. Hezekiah found a way to do both.

The story is told in the Bible Books of Kings and Chronicles. 'Hezekiah . . . took counsel with his princes and his mighty men to stop the waters of the fountains which were without the city . . . This same Hezekiah also stopped the upper watercourse of Gihon and brought it straight down to the west side of the city of David.' A short tunnel leading from the Gihon spring perhaps enabled David, as we have seen, to capture the city from the Jebusites three hundred years earlier. Hezekiah's engineers now blocked up all the springs outside the walls except one. Sealing up the cave entrance to

OPPOSITE The
Temple platform seen
from the Mount of
Olives, showing the
golden Dome of the
Rock built by the
Muslims after their
capture of Jerusalem
in the seventh century
AD. Beneath the dome
is the sacred rock
which may have
supported the altar of
burnt sacrifice in
Solomon's day.

64

the spring of Gihon, they diverted its waters through an extended tunnel under the city walls to a place on lower ground where it made a pool, the Pool of Siloam, out of sight and fear of Assyrian attack.

In his Gospel, St John tells the story of a man who, seven centuries after Hezekiah, was born blind. Jesus put a plaster of mud and spittle on his eyes and then told him, 'Go wash in the Pool of Siloam' and the man 'washed and came seeing'. In 1880 AD an Arab boy, playing with his friend at the Pool of Siloam, fell in, and groping his way out made a momentous discovery. On the far side of the pool rose a rock wall, and here the boy saw there was a passage about two feet wide and five feet high. Scholars, whose attention was drawn to the discovery, probed a few feet inside and there found a Hebrew inscription. It read:

> 'The boring through is completed. And this is the story of the boring: while yet they plied the pick, each toward his fellow, and while yet there were three cubits ($4\frac{1}{2}$ feet) to be bored through, there was heard the voice of one calling to the other that there was a hole in the rock on the right hand and on the left hand. And on the day of the boring through the workers in the tunnel struck each to meet his fellow, pick upon pick. Then the water poured from the source to the pool 1200 cubits (600 yards) and 100 cubits was the height of the rock above the heads of the workers in the tunnel.'

This was Hezekiah's aqueduct.

And yet, it seems, the safe and secret water supply was not enough —nor were Isaiah's exhortations enough—to steel Jerusalem to total defiance of Sennacherib. The Assyrian used a form of psychological warfare in advance of that employed by Joshua at Jericho five centuries earlier. He sent propagandists—men who spoke the local language— to the city to persuade the people that resistance was useless and could lead only to death from hunger and thirst. They distributed a message from Sennacherib himself asserting that their God could no more save them than He had saved other cities that had fallen to his army. Isaiah struck back, urging the people to be 'not afraid of the words which thou hast heard'. Then, strangely enough on the face of it, the people looking over the walls saw the enemy strike camp and disappear. As suggested in an earlier chapter, perhaps Hezekiah saved himself by agreeing to pay tribute and was saved in a later siege by a mysterious disaster to Sennacherib's army.

Jerusalem's next trial came at the turn of the sixth century, when

*Above* The northern end of the Siloam Tunnel in Jerusalem. *Below* Jewish crowds at the western wall of the Temple platform, 'the Wailing Wall', after the Israeli Army captured the Old City in 1967.

65

Judah became a vassal state of Nebuchadrezzar. Judah, like a disgruntled tenant holding back his rent, stopped paying tribute levied by Babylon, and in 597 BC Nebuchadrezzar descended on Jerusalem to enforce his claim. He sent to Babylon as captives the 18-year-old king Jehoiachin, the queen mother, members of leading families and skilled workers, and left the king's uncle Zedekiah as chastened caretaker of the denuded city. This is the Bible story, and as we have seen, the world had to wait 2,500 years for corroboration in records from Nebuchadrezzar's own capital in cuneiform tablets unearthed by the German expedition of Robert Koldewey.

Zedekiah, after nine years as a puppet, and urged on by young Judean nationalists (but against the warnings of the prophet Jeremiah), was pushed into a new revolt. It failed and this time Nebuchadrezzar's vengeance was terrible. He laid siege to Jerusalem for eighteen months until starvation broke the spirit of the people. Zedekiah himself then made a desperate attempt to escape by leaving the city with a bodyguard by a gate near the royal gardens under cover of night. They were seen: the Babylonians overtook the fugitive party on the plains of Jericho when they had gone barely a dozen miles; and they brought Zedekiah back to face Nebuchadrezzar. The Babylonians first executed Zedekiah's children before his eyes and then blinded him. Then Nebuchadrezzar turned his soldiers loose on Jerusalem. The palace was plundered, the Temple destroyed, the city walls broken down, and 'all the houses of Jerusalem' smashed to rubble. More deportations to slave labour swelled the number of exiles in Babylon, mocked by their foreign masters with the demand, 'Sing us one of the songs of Zion.' This was the end of the commonwealth of Judah.

Modern archaeologists have found a striking extra measurement of Nebuchadrezzar's wrath, showing that other towns and fortresses suffered Babylonian destruction at the same time. But the great loss was Jerusalem. For it means that nothing of the cities of David or Solomon, except the sites, could afterwards be found. And yet, paradoxically, more of it is still there than remains of other Biblical cities which did not endure the same savagery but were built of sunbaked mud bricks in places where there is little or no stone. Jerusalem has abundant stone, and when buildings collapsed or were destroyed by enemy action, the stone could be used again and again, not necessarily on the same site. In 1962 exploration uncovered outside the shaft to Hezekiah's water tunnel the massive boulder foundations of walls built before the Jebusite occupation.

A tumble of stones on the steep terraced eastern slope of ancient Jerusalem in the area where Nehemiah, surveying the city destroyed by Nebuchadrezzar, found his donkey's path blocked with rubble.

They remained the town walls under David and for several centuries afterwards, because the rock at its foot was shown to have been kept clear for three hundred years after David's reign. But what fragments of David's and Solomon's and Zedekiah's Jerusalem may lie in latter-day house walls and foundations is beyond reckoning.

When Cyrus the Persian overthrew the Babylonian power and allowed the Jews after many years of captivity to return to Jerusalem and restore their Temple, he also ordered that all the gold and silver ornaments looted by Nebuchadrezzar be returned to the new house of the Lord. Under the influence of Ezra the priest, the Jews divorced their foreign wives and pledged themselves anew to the law of Moses: under the leadership of Nehemiah, who had been a courtier in exile but was appointed Governor of Jerusalem on his return in about 440 BC, they set about restoring a dilapidated city.

In the Old Testament Book of Nehemiah, Nehemiah himself describes how he went out at night-time with a few picked men and surveyed the ruined gates and walls, and on his return, exhorted the people to build. A number of aliens jeered, and asked, 'What are you doing—planning a fresh revolt against the king?' And Nehemiah answered: 'The God of Heaven, he will prosper us: therefore we his servants will arise and build; but ye have no portion, nor right, nor memorial, in Jerusalem.' The inspired Jews fell to the task with fanatical zeal, working so hard that 'neither I (says Nehemiah) nor my brethren, nor my servants, nor the men of the guard . . . none of us put off our clothes, saving that everyone put them off for washing.' The Bible says that rebuilding the walls took only 52 days—an incredible feat unless Nehemiah's walled Jerusalem was smaller even than Solomon's.

It was a curious incident on Nehemiah's nocturnal survey that gave modern archaeologists a clue to where to look for Nehemiah's walls. Nehemiah had reported that as he rode around and reached 'the King's Pool' (now thought to be the present-day Pool of Siloam) he found his way blocked, for 'there was no room for the beast that was under me to pass'. The reference to a blockage was intriguing— because here on the steep western slope of the Kidron Valley, houses were built on artificial terraces of stone; it was a perilous system, for if any of the lower houses were destroyed by an enemy or fell down in the heavy spring rains, this was liable to cause the higher terraces right up to the crest of the hill to collapse in an avalanche. Modern explorers have found deep piles of debris from such avalanches, and it was evidently some early portion of this that had barred the way for Nehemiah's donkey. The archaeologist Kathleen Kenyon reasoned that Nehemiah had therefore abandoned the idea of rebuilding on the slope, and had instead retracted the eastern perimeter to the crest of the hill. And sure enough, when her excavators came to dig, they discovered walls on the eastern crest and debris at its outer base, datable to the fifth to fourth century BC—that is, to the time of Nehemiah.

No written records give a reliable picture of Jerusalem in the century that ended when the Persian empire fell in 332 BC to the brilliant young general from Macedonia who became Alexander the Great. Alexander did not harm Jerusalem, but the inheritors of the nearby part of his empire did. These were the Seleucids, the so-called 'Greeks of Syria', whose first king, Seleucus I, had served as a general under Alexander. Having routed the Greeks of Egypt in 198 BC, they sought to impose the worship of Greek gods, defiled the Temple with pagan sacrifices, and at length drove the Jews to such anger and despair that they rose in revolt. Out of the revolt came the short-lived Jewish control of their own holy city under the Maccabee kings. It lasted 120 years and the Romans put an end to that independence in 63 BC.

Herod, the Edomite from the south, whom the Romans put in charge of this new piece of their empire, was a sinister figure—a lustful man who married ten women and died of venereal disease, ruthless in the pursuit and preservation of power (the New Testament says that in his time were massacred small children when the forecast of a Saviour's birth was seen as a distant threat to his throne), a jealous killer who did not hesitate to put his own sons to death. But he was also an excellent administrator and—the only important characteristic for archaeology—a great builder. One of his enterprises was the creation of a palace in Jerusalem close to today's Jaffa Gate in the western wall of the Old City. It had three towers dedicated to the memory of his brother Phasael, his friend Hippicus, and his wife Mariamne—the one he had loved best but murdered when he was falsely informed that she had been unfaithful to him. All that is left today is the base of the Phasael Tower, stones more than four cubic feet each and set without mortar. This is known today erroneously as David's Tower: in 1961 stone filling in the tower base was recognised to be debris from ruined houses of the seventh century BC— three hundred years later than David—and clearly a tower built over such ruins could not possibly be of David's time.

In the north, but well inside the walls, Herod built a fortress and called it Antonia in flattery of his Roman patron Mark Antony. According to the historian Josephus it contained 'every kind of dwelling and other convenience, colonnades, baths and broad courts for encampments, so that in possessing all manner of utilities it seemed a city, but in sumptuousness, a palace.' Only a few remains of it have been uncovered in modern times.

But the building on which Herod lavished most care and money was the Temple. He reconstructed it with its holiest part on the same ground plan as Solomon's, but with its buildings soaring even higher and its precincts of a huge porch, cloisters and courtyards spreading beyond it. Herod extended Solomon's site, which lay immediately south of the Antonia fortress, by building an immense platform 400 yards long by 300 yards broad—somewhat larger than London's Trafalgar Square—and supported it with great buttress walls rising on the eastern side from the Kidron Valley and on the west from the Tyropoeon Valley, which was very deep in those days but has since filled up with debris to form the shallow depression of today. He used 10,000 labourers for the task, begun in 20 BC and finished only many years after his death. He even went to the length of training 1,000 priests as masons and carpenters to build those parts of the sanctuary which profane hands were not allowed to touch. The front was faced with gold-plated white stone so that from a

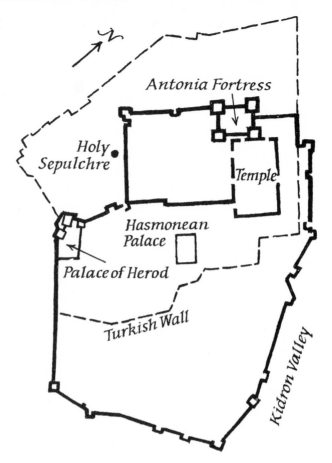

The main buildings
of Herod's Jerusalem

distance it shone in the sunlight 'like a mountain covered with snow'.

Surrounding the whole complex was a massive wall. It had numerous gates (four in the west, according to Josephus) which provided access to the upper city. Two of them gave on to arching viaducts over the western valley. The Talmud, which emerged out of oral traditions of the Jews over many centuries and is their main source of religion after the Bible, said of the grand design: 'He who has not set eyes upon the structure of Herod has not seen a structure of beauty in all his life.'

This was the Jerusalem of Jesus; the courtyards of the Temple were where he held his brief ministry, and not far away was the place where he was executed. Pontius Pilate, who provided his death warrant, made his headquarters at Caesarea on the Mediterranean coast—the Romans wanted to diminish the importance of Jerusalem as a possible focal point of Jewish mutiny. The procurators visited Jerusalem from time to time, especially on Jewish festival days because these drew in many worshippers from the countryside. The danger that religious fervour would explode into defiance and revolt against the pagan Roman masters was greater on such days. It was on one of these visits that Pilate yielded to the crucifixion of Jesus. The festival was the Passover, which marks Jewish folk memory of the Exodus from bondage in Egypt. It was celebrated by Jews then—as now—in late March or April by a special meal at which they ate bitter herbs to symbolise the harshness of their slavery in Egypt; the sacrificial lamb whose blood was sprinkled on doorposts of Israelite homes just before the Exodus so that the Angel of Death would 'pass over' them; unleavened bread which signified the haste of the departure from Egypt—no time to wait for the dough to rise—and ritual wine. This was the meal Jesus ate with his disciples that night in the spring of 33 AD: the Last Supper, out of which grew the Roman Catholic Mass and the Anglican celebration of Holy Communion. In Jerusalem you may walk in the 'upper room' where the supper is traditionally supposed to have been eaten. But the Gospels say only that Jesus asked his disciples to go into the city and follow a man they would see with a pitcher of water, and to enter the house he entered, and there they would sup. So there is no certainty today where the meal was eaten and the room shown to visitors is part of a building built 1,300 years later than the Crucifixion.

Christ has left no material traces on earth and archaeologists know that all they can do is reconstruct the environment of the time in which he lived, taught and died. There is dispute over the place where he was sentenced to death: some think it was in Herod's palace on the south-west hill near the Jaffa Gate; others think it was in the Antonia fortress near the Temple on the eastern hill. Tourists today walk along the Via Dolorosa, but the route Christ actually stumbled over, carrying his cross to the scene of his lingering death on Calvary outside the city walls, remains unproved. Wherever the path was, it now lies deep under the surface, hidden by centuries of debris: and yet perhaps not quite all. Alongside the Via Dolorosa, in a Christian nunnery, you can see, well below the present street level, blood red marble paving stones on which Roman soldiers scratched out geometric designs for some gambling game; so perhaps this authentic Roman level is part of Christ's path.

Bible guidance on where Jesus walked the night before he died is

more precise. After supper, according to St Mark, he left the house in the city and went to the Mount of Olives, where on warm nights he slept and prayed with his followers. To do this, he and his disciples would have to cross the Kidron Valley and climb a little way up the farther slope to the piece of ground called Gethsemane. This is where Jesus, knowing his earthly doom was near, spent the dark hours among the olive trees, praying for strength to endure the coming ordeal. Olive trees still clothe the hillside and today the Franciscan monks maintain a tiny garden where, in the fifteenth century, the olive trees were already old. It may well be that they grew from shoots from the trees which Christ knew and which were cut down a few years after his death when the Romans sacked Jerusalem in 70 AD.

Apart from some fragments the only visible survival of the flame and battery of the Roman general Titus is the great Temple platform, today graced with the Dome of the Rock, one of the most beautiful buildings in the world, and Al Aqsa mosque, both of which are Muslim houses of prayer built during the 400-year occupation of Palestine by Arab power that began in 636 AD.

The walls that now enclose the Old City were rebuilt between 1538 and 1541 AD by the Turk, Suleiman the Magnificent, but along the eastern edge of the Temple platform they are Herodian from the base until near the top, and also on the western side, whence viaducts reached out to link the Temple complex with Herod's royal quarters across the Tyropoeon Valley on the western hill. The roots of one bridge, called Robinson's Arch after its discoverer, are visible today, and part of the other, Wilson's Arch, also named after its discoverer, is a complete barrel vault that can be reached below ground.

This Herodian western wall is called the Wailing Wall, because after the Romans destroyed the Temple they first barred Jews from setting foot even in the ruins, but later relented and permitted Jews once a year to return to mourn over its stones. The Jews were once more barred access to this last remnant of their holiest shrine when modern Israel was created in 1948. At the cease-fire it lay in Jordanian hands. All the greater on that account was the emotion of Jewry nineteen years later when Israeli troops stormed the gates of the Old City in the Six Day War of 1967. Crowds flocked to the Wailing Wall with the soldiers, all weeping with hysterical joy and kissing the worn old stones.

For archaeology the destruction of 70 AD was not the last calamity that struck Jerusalem. On the ruins the Roman Emperor Hadrian

Excavations at the southern wall of the Temple platform uncovered stones that had crashed down onto a paved street when the Romans destroyed the Temple in 70 AD.

founded a new heathen city named Aelia Capitolina (Aelia after Hadrian's family name, and Capitolina after the highest of the seven hills of Rome on which stood the temple of Jupiter). And he quarried the southern site of the capital of David and Solomon for the building stone he needed. The result was not only to bury under new buildings the Jerusalem of Herod and Jesus, which lay on the site of Aelia Capitolina, but to destroy the foundations of the earliest Jerusalem. Subsequent occupation has, of course, severely restricted the opportunity to dig beneath the present built-on skin which obliterates the Jerusalem of the New Testament. Nevertheless, every now and again something new—or rather, something very old—turns up. Since 1968 excavators have uncovered more Herodian buildings in the western wall, and also in the southern wall. At a depth of ten courses of stone and 39 feet they came upon a paved road beneath the southern wall, and there they found fresh evidence of the skill and enterprise of Herod's engineers, for some of the masonry blocks were thirty feet long; one weighed a hundred tons. They also laid bare—for the first time in 1,900 years—stones that had crashed down on a paved street when the Romans demolished the Temple in 70 AD. In January 1970 workmen confirmed that the destruction had been accompanied by fire; their spades struck the charred remains of Jerusalem homes in which were found coins that had been minted during the Jewish revolt of 66 AD.

In May 1971, contractors digging foundations for an Armenian theological seminary in the walled city, came upon remains which the Israeli Department of Antiquities identified as part of Herod's palace.

# 5

# The Masada Tragedy

Travel down the dark ribbon of road south of Jerusalem in summer, and on either hand you may see Ruth—as Boaz saw her in the Bethlehem fields 3,000 years ago—working in the corn, black-robed and shy as she still is in the twentieth century. Or earlier in the year, after the February and March rains that vein the valleys with flash floods, you will see the undulating land on the edge of the desert become a quilt of pale flowers growing so thickly it looks as if the storms had brushed the earth with a film of snow. But westward from the town of Arad the landscape breaks up into sand and gravel, rocky heights and raw ravines; and here, any time after April, the sun burns down with a heat and pressure pleasurable only to the lizards jerking their heads into its glare.

Along this road in the year 70 AD straggled the remnants of a people. They were Jews from Jerusalem. Four years earlier they had rebelled against Rome. They faced heavy odds, but they hoped for an intervention by God that never came. The Romans put down their revolt, destroyed their Temple in Jerusalem, slaughtered or enslaved thousands of prisoners, and marched south to snuff out the last embers of rebellion. Fervent Jewish nationalists were forced to surrender strongholds at Machaerus, where John the Baptist was executed, and at Herodion, near Bethlehem, where Herod was buried. Now the remainder, known to history as Zealots, were trekking farther south to join another resistance group which had been entrenched on the rock of Masada since the start of the revolt, and which had since harried the local Roman forces on the western shores of the Dead Sea.

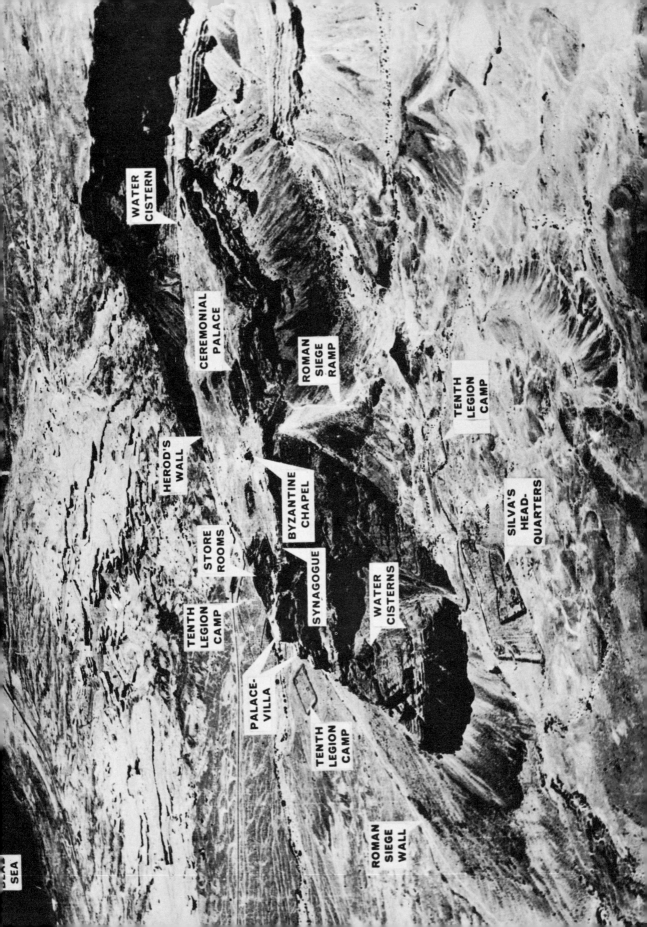

WATER
CISTERN

CEREMONIAL
PALACE

ROMAN
SIEGE
RAMP

TENTH
LEGION
CAMP

HEROD'S
WALL

BYZANTINE
CHAPEL

STORE
ROOMS

SYNAGOGUE

SILVA'S
HEAD-
QUARTERS

WATER
CISTERNS

TENTH
LEGION
CAMP

PALACE-
VILLA

TENTH
LEGION
CAMP

DEAD
SEA

ROMAN
SIEGE
WALL

Masada, its bulk heaved up out of a lunar-like landscape, must have had the same time-worn, exhausted look it has today. About it there hangs an air of mystery and horror that suits the drama that was then about to unfold. Its flat top of about 23 acres, shaped like the deck of a ship, had been a fortified place in the days of the Maccabee kings. 'Jonathan the High Priest' is said to have been the first to fortify the rock at some unknown date, but the man who turned it into a real citadel was Herod the Great.

Herod ruled Judea as a vassal of Rome for 37 years until his death at the age of seventy in the year of Christ's birth. History books give the life span of Herod as about 73 BC to 4 BC according to the chronology introduced by the sixth-century scholar Dionysius Exiguus and still current, but it is widely accepted that Dionysius wrongly dated the birth of Christ. Herod fortified Masada because of fears that he might need a secure refuge if his Jewish subjects ever rebelled, or if his Roman overlords replaced him. Perhaps the second fear was the stronger one, and the reason for this went back to an upheaval in Rome four years before the Senate had appointed him.

In 44 BC Brutus and Cassius and their fellow conspirators had murdered Julius Caesar, and two years later, at Philippi in Greece, Caesar's friends Antony and Octavian defeated the forces of the assassins. Thereafter the eastern half of Rome's colonial territories, including Palestine, came under Antony's control. He made his headquarters in Egypt, and fell deeply in love with the Egyptian queen Cleopatra. Herod knew that Cleopatra coveted Judea for herself, and he was afraid that one day Antony would give it to her.

So between the years 36 and 30 BC Herod built up Masada as a place of retreat in case of disaster. He surrounded the summit with towers and a wall. He dammed a valley to catch the flash floods, and from the dam, by an ingenious system of aqueducts, steered the water into cisterns cut into the rock face about half way up the sides of Masada. These enormous chambers could hold more than nine million gallons of water each. Even under siege conditions they could be reached by dizzy paths from the summit. But their apertures and the aqueducts were visible—and therefore vulnerable—to an enemy. So, having excavated the cisterns, Herod dug new ones into the rock on the summit itself. These his slaves must have filled laboriously with buckets or skin bottles from the cisterns in the sides of the cliff.

Herod, like the Romans, loved baths. He built large and small ones on Masada. And he built himself palaces; one close to the western walls where he had his throne room and administrative offices, the other a three-terrace pleasure villa on the northern tip of the precipice. The lowest and most beautiful terrace was built on vast buttresses reaching up from the face of the rock, so that it seems to anyone walking on the terrace to be suspended in the void. With its fluted pillars and painted plaster panels and its breath-taking views, it must have been in Herod's day the most sumptuous and spectacular gazebo in the world. Here he could sit with his guests and friends in the only place on Masada completely protected from the savage heat of the sun and the searing desert winds, and look out over the salt-heavy disc of sea below and the dead cliffs and mountains around as far as the barriers of the mountains of Moab.

Herod's twin fears never came to anything in his own life time. But seventy years after his death the first of them occurred—rebellion by the Jews. When the Romans had destroyed Jerusalem and stamped out the revolt over the rest of the land, they decided they could no longer tolerate the defiance of the resistance group on Masada, now joined by the Zealots from Jerusalem, a single sore spot on the map whose infection might inflame the whole colony into fresh outbreaks. Masada held by the Jews was also an affront to the efficiency of the rule of Flavius Silva, now Procurator of Judea. Silva was a soldier. He put himself at the head of the celebrated Tenth Legion and inflated its strength with auxiliary troops and thousands of prisoner-slaves carrying water, timber and provisions across the barren plateau. He knew the nature of his enemy, for he had been one of the commanders at the siege of Jerusalem. When he reached Masada late in 72 AD he built eight siege camps and a containing wall, two miles long and six feet thick, all round the rock. He meant no Jew to escape.

The only source for what happened next is an account by Josephus Flavius, the contemporary Jewish historian. Josephus knew the background to the revolt; he had been part of it as a Jewish commander in Galilee, but at a critical moment he had gone over to the Romans as a collaborator.

From the eastern side the walls of Masada were impregnable, for they fall almost sheer for about 1,300 feet towards the shores of the Dead Sea, and there is no cover an attacking force could take. Silva saw that he would have to strike from the western side where the walls are less daunting and where a spur against them links the rock

Cosmetic equipment
excavated at Masada

with the broad Judean plain. Opposite the spur Silva set up his headquarters camp, and against the walls he began to build a gigantic ramp. You may see it today, pointing like a white, stubby-bladed dagger at the heart of Masada. Indeed, you may walk up the blade and see, protruding from the sloping edges, the ends of ancient timbers embedded there by Silva's engineers to hold the rock and gravel of the ramp together: a striking monument to Roman military engineering skill.

And there came a day in the spring of 73 AD when Eleazar ben Ya'ir, leader of the Zealot garrison of 967 men, women and children, looked down from the walls of Masada and looked down upon their doom. The ramp was finished and the Romans were about to storm the walls. They mounted a tower on a platform built on top of the ramp so that they could hurl stones and arrows *down* on the defenders whilst other units of the Legion directed battering rams against the walls.

Josephus reports that Eleazar ben Ya'ir assembled his band of diehards, and knowing that the end must be near, exhorted them to take their own lives rather than surrender. Josephus, in the manner of historians of his time, puts heroic words into the mouth of Eleazar:

'It has been, my friends, the custom with the people of our nation to deny authority of every other lord save the great sovereign of the universe, the eternal God; and this we have done without excepting the Romans or anyone else. The time has now come when we must demonstrate our sincerity by our conduct: wherefore let us act like men of resolution. Till this time we have run every risk in preservation of our freedom; but we must now expect thralldom and tormenting punishments if the enemy take us alive, since we first departed from their dominion and have been the last to resist them. We may deem it a favour if we are permitted to choose the death we would die . . .

'We shall be made slaves tomorrow if we obtain not our liberty this night. But this we may do in a way that our enemies cannot prevent . . . Thus acting, we should secure the honour of our wives and protect our children from slavery. Let us . . . make our own terms and die. But first let us set fire to the fortress and to our possessions; and thus the Romans, neither taking us prisoner nor finding anything to loot, will even regret the possession of the place . . . Only let us spare our food store, to serve as proof

OPPOSITE The rock
of Masada, with
Herod the Great's
three-tiered palace-
villa on the northern
tip.

that we were not driven to this violent procedure by famine, but
maintained our first resolution of dying rather than submitting
to slavery . . . Let us die free men, gloriously surrounded by our
wives and children. And let us be expeditious. Eternal renown
shall be ours by snatching the prize from the hands of the enemy,
and leaving him nothing to triumph over but the bodies of those
who dared to be their own executioners . . .'

It is beyond our capacity at this distance of time to imagine the
state of mind of a people faced with such a terrible proposal. We are
more familiar with history's instances of people at the point of
despair, fighting, as an animal does, for survival when all hope of
survival has gone. One thinks of the Spartans fighting to the last
man at Thermopylae, or of the embattled Texans at the Alamo.
Perhaps out of their tragic history the Jews have developed inside
themselves a greater than normal human share of fatalism. Josephus
records that six years earlier, when the troops of Vespasian, the
father of Titus, besieged the city of Gamala near Tiberius, more than
5,000 Jews 'despairing of escape, and hemmed in every way . . .
flung their wives and children and themselves too into the immensely
deep ravine that yawned under the citadel.' In the eleventh century
AD, when a group of Jews in England were threatened with extermina-
tion they all killed themselves in a tower in York. At Masada the
garrison responded to Eleazar's exhortation, for as Josephus wrote,
the married men slew their families; then lots were cast, and ten
men were chosen to kill the rest of the garrison; and then, casting
lots afresh, one was chosen to despatch the other nine before taking
his own life by the sword. But before the mass suicide was over
they set fire to Masada. When the Romans burst through the walls
they walked into smoking ruins and the silence of the dead.

Josephus tells how they reacted to their conquest.

'When they came upon the rows of dead bodies, they did not
exult over their enemies, but admired the nobility of their resolve,
and the way in which so many had shown, in carrying it out
without a tremor, an utter contempt for death.'

How, one may ask, did Josephus know the details of this tragic
story? He was not there when it happened. The answer given is
that two women and five children hid from the killing and survived
to tell about it. It is also possible that Josephus spoke with Romans
who took part in the final assault.

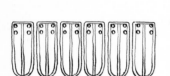

Silvered scales of
armour found near
the skeleton of a
Zealot warrior

Let us, for a few moments, jump the next 1,850 years to the twentieth century and a new resistance movement in Palestine. It was called the Haganah, which means 'Defence'. It was formed by Jewish settlers, first against hostile Arabs and then against the occupying troops of the British who ruled Palestine as League of Nations trustees, and who declared it illegal for more than a certain quota of Jewish immigrants to enter Palestine. In the ranks of the Haganah in 1931 was a messenger boy called Yigael Sukenik. His parents were immigrants: they had trekked from Poland as young Zionists and teachers in 1912, and his father had become Palestine's first Jewish Professor of Archaeology at the Hebrew University in Jerusalem. Young Sukenik soon became an active guerrilla leader. His code name in the Haganah was Yadin. In Hebrew it means 'He who will judge', and his judgements were such that before he was out of his twenties he was Haganah's chief of planning operations. And when war between Arabs and Jews broke out in 1948, he emerged with the Haganah—now called the Defence Force of Israel—as its 31-year-old Chief of Staff.

Sukenik believed that the most dangerous enemy would be the ancient enemy of Egypt, and he directed Israeli forces south against them. He called his offensive Operation Ten Plagues—after the Bible story of the ten plagues or disasters brought upon Egypt by God through Moses when Pharaoh refused to set free Sukenik's persecuted ancestors.

At some point in this campaign the Egyptian forces in the desert commanded the only two known roads of communication. Sukenik, who always wanted to be an archaeologist like his father, carried in his baggage ancient as well as modern maps. And when an impasse was reached in the desert he remembered that in the days of the Roman Empire there had been a third road. He checked his maps afresh, then ordered his field commander to send out scouts. They went out, prodding through the sand in the area he had indicated, and they found the third road. It was, of course, masked with centuries of blown sand, and the Israelis moved along it with extreme caution, fearing that if they got any wheeled vehicle off the paved surface they would be lost in the sand. It took them sixteen hours to cover the first four miles. But in the end they turned the unsuspecting Egyptian flank, took the enemy completely by surprise, and captured their staff officers—including a brigadier dressed only in his pyjamas. The impasse was broken. Sukenik was a hero, and as his kinsmen saw it, a hero in the most glorious of all contexts, a war of independence.

One of the huge cisterns which supplied water to Masada, excavated from solid rock by Herod the Great's engineers. A sunbeam streams through the hole below the ceiling through which water was poured to fill the cistern from flood-water catchment cisterns in the sides of Masada.

81

Professor Yigael Yadin, leader of the 1963–5 expedition, on the walls of Masada. In the distance below are the remains of the Tenth Legion's camp headquarters.

On the day of victory the leaders of the new State of Israel met and decided to mark the new era in their people's history by taking real Hebrew names. Yigael Sukenik thus became Yigael Yadin. But with the war over and won Yadin took the first opportunity to turn himself back into an archaeologist—with the remarkable result that his subsequent exploits as an archaeologist had the same spectacular quality as his feats of war. In the nineteen-fifties at Hazor in northern Galilee he led a team of explorers who unearthed buildings of Solomon and laid bare the tracks of Joshua. In 1963 he was ready to dig into the secrets of Masada.

After its recapture by the Romans in 73 AD the ruined fortress had passed into near oblivion. In the fifth or sixth century after Christ a group of Christian monks built a chapel on the summit, using dressed stones from the remains of Herodian and Zealot buildings. But how and whence they came, who they really were and when they left, is not known. It was not until 1838 that Masada was identified again as the scene of the mass suicide. In that year an American scholar, Edward Robinson, and a companion, H. Smith, travelling across the desert, looked through a telescope at a distant rock which the local Arabs called Sebbeh. They noticed a cluster of ruins on what seemed to be a totally inaccessible summit. Smith felt sure this must be the site of 'the ancient and renowned fortress of Masada'. And so it was.

Later travellers sketched and then scaled the rock. Archaeologists followed them and found astonishing accuracy in Josephus's description. But Masada was not thoroughly mapped between Herod's time and 1955, and even then nobody possessed both the determination and the resources to dig up its secrets.

The basic needs were substantial funds, a reliable labour force, water and food in a desert that provided neither, and transport across a trackless waste. The absence of one or more of these necessities limited the scope of all archaeological pioneers in Bible lands in the nineteenth century; the difficulty of obtaining all four in the twentieth century was the main reason why Masada remained a locked treasure house until 1963.

In that year, however, there was assembled the best-equipped expedition hitherto seen in Palestine. It became a classic exercise in method and planning. It was led by Yadin, who now held the chair of archaeology at the Hebrew University in Jerusalem that his father had held before him. He obtained copious financial support from two distinguished British families—Mrs Harry Sacher, her sister Mrs Terence Kennedy, and the Wolfson Foundation— and the support of *The Observer* newspaper. And he also had the backing of his own people, in particular the Defence Force of Israel. Army engineers blasted a road for twenty miles across the wilderness from the new town of Arad, built a fire-escape style staircase up the last hundred feet or so of the cliff face from the top of Silva's ramp, and provided helicopters for initial aerial survey. Israel's national water company piped water to the site; trucks brought food daily from Arad to be reheated in camp kitchens.

The remaining vital need began to be met within 24 hours of the appearance in *The Observer* on Sunday, 13 August, of an invitation to the world for volunteers. Applicants were told they must be prepared to make their own way to Israel and as far south as Beersheba. They must agree to work for at least fourteen days. These days would be hot and the work hard; the nights cold in unheated tents, sleeping ten to each tent. Food would be simple and adequate, but that was all. There would be no pay for their labour, and they would have to devise their own entertainment for spare time in the desert.

The response was a startling measurement of the spread of public interest in archaeology in this century. The early pioneers—men like Rawlinson and Rich, Layard and Woolley—would have been astonished to see what they had started. There was a postal avalanche of applications: in the end more than 5,000 from 28 different countries.

83

They came from men and women, old and young, rich and poor. There were company directors ready to leave their boardrooms, clerks and students, plumbers, painters, lorry drivers, nurses, doctors, secretaries, dentists, engineers, artists, gardeners, waiters, book-sellers, lawyers. There was a shepherdess from the Canary Islands, a fashion model from Australia, a bookmaker's clerk from Grimsby, an elephant tamer, and even a middle-aged woman who rather desperately listed midwifery among her possibly desirable skills.

They sailed across the Atlantic, flew from New Zealand, motored from Scandinavia, hitch-hiked from all over Europe. Some wanted to wrench themselves out of their office prisons; some sought adventure for its own sake; some were trying to seize a heaven-sent chance to see the Bible lands that had been no nearer than Sunday school picture books; some had not begun their adult lives and were searching for a signpost; others were grasping what seemed to be one of the rapidly diminishing opportunities left in the world to become involved in activity from which there was no personal or political advantage to be gained. In many the stronger impulse to give than to gain was obvious. A London salesman who pleaded to take his sixteen-year-old son to Masada (the age limit fixed by the expedition was seventeen) wrote to Yadin: 'My object is partly educational, but mainly that my son may be shown by example to give of his time and labour without financial reward for the joy of worthwhile endeavour alongside young people of other nations.'

Yadin recruited two staffs, one of archaeologists and the other of administrators, to run the camp organisation. The archaeologists were themselves divided into two teams, one directly in charge of excavations, each member having control of a section of the summit of the rock and the volunteers digging there, the other of technicians such as draughtsmen to superintend drawings of all finds, the official photographer, pottery restorers and so on. The total expedition force averaged two hundred people at any one time. The chosen volunteers for fortnightly shifts arrived at Masada in work-forces of between fifty and eighty, with groups of thirty Israeli soldiers lent by the Army, and groups of forty to fifty young Israelis doing their compulsory national service. All were first lectured on the story of Masada and what the expedition hoped to find, then taken on a guided tour of the site, and finally split into sections to work on the summit in fixed areas or at the base camp.

The surface of Masada and its neighbourhood had already been divided in the aerial survey into sections one hundred metres square, numbered from east to west and north to south. Each square was then sub-divided into a hundred smaller squares. These were marked from east to west by letters and from north to south by numbers. Work teams were allotted to numbered squares under a leader, and everything they found was carefully marked. Thus, 5–16/2 meant meant that object No 2, in basket No 16, was found in area No 5. The different layers of excavation were also numbered as work proceeded. The top of Masada was thus peeled off, as it were skin by skin, and as the dust and debris of history passed through the work teams' sieves, nothing was lost, nothing was overlooked, and every significant fragment down to the size of a bean was recovered and recorded.

The expedition's day was also precisely scheduled: reveille at five a.m. before sun-up, teams up the ramp to begin work on the summit at six, each member carrying a bag of bread and cheese and oranges for a second breakfast break at nine; lunch (brought up the rock on a small wire-rope railway) at twelve; and a halt at three p.m. The volunteers were then free for showers, an evening meal in the communal dining tent, film shows afterwards or music-making sessions in their own and neighbouring tents. The archaeological staff's section leaders, however, met each evening round a table in the administrative quarters, chewing nuts or sunflower seeds from little heaps set before them, and reporting to Yadin in turn on the day's discoveries. Each report was tape-recorded and then typed for a complete written record.

During the day all the baskets of finds were transported on the wire-rope system down the rock to sorting sheds and washing places. All finds were photographed, drawn to scale, numbered, card-indexed, and stored or set aside for restoration if the finds were fragments of vessels and other artifacts that could be put together again.

Professor Yadin believed that if the Zealots were unwilling to surrender their lives to the Romans, they would be equally unwilling to surrender the sacred documents of their faith. It is not the custom of Jews to burn or spoil any sacred writing. Such scriptures are buried, like bodies, if they must be got rid of. Masada also held the promise of an archaeological bonus. For the fire which destroyed Masada would serve to give a precise dating to anything that survived. It would not be necessary to say of a discovered necklace or wine jar, 'This comes from a period roughly at the time of Christ, give a couple of centuries either way.' Anything found of a Jewish nature must date from the Jewish occupation which lasted less than seven

Volunteers at their midday break, looking out towards the Dead Sea in the distance. In the foreground are some of the baskets in which all finds were lowered from the summit of Masada to the base camp for examination and classification.

years, and nothing found beneath the black ashes of the fire could be later in date than 73 AD.

The expedition got under way in October 1963 when the summer heat had abated, and it first tackled the northern edge, where Herod the Great built his fantastic three-tier hanging palace—fantastic because its third and lowest terrace, supported on the great buttress built into the face of the cliff where no natural foundations were possible, is rather like a martin's nest clinging to the sheer wall of a house: a marvel of mathematical calculation and building skill. Behind the top terrace, and athwart the narrow northern neck of the rock, lay an elongated mound with a crest of stones from east to west, sealing off the palace from the rest of the plateau. It looked like the top of a wall. The digging began here and continued until 40,000 cubic metres of debris had been shifted. It contained the fragments of hundreds of vessels. The 1963 work teams were in effect, dustmen for Masada's Herodian, Roman and Zealot communal rubbish dump. And what lay revealed was a deep wall of white stucco—a vast screen to shield the privacy of Herod's villa palace from the prying eyes of his army of servants and slaves, and even his own military guard.

Other work teams moved into the palace beyond the screen wall. On the top terrace they found Herod's living quarters, the floors paved with black and white mosaics—the earliest mosaics found in

86

Israel—and rooms built round a courtyard. A steep secret passage descended to the middle terrace. Here were two circular walls, each three and a half feet thick, one inside the other with a space of four feet in between. Nineteenth-century travellers had talked of a round tower and a 'strong circular fort with double walls'. But what purpose could there be here for a fort or a tower perched on the edge of a quite inaccessible cliff? None. The tops of the circular walls were smooth and level: they had never been any higher. What, in fact, the explorers had found was the support for the circular floor of what must have been a splendid colonnaded pavilion: they could see where the ends of beams had fitted into the rock face at the back of it. It was Herod's engineers' brilliant answer to the problem of building the pavilion he wanted on the face of a cliff which left them no room for massive foundations. A single circular wall filled with rubble might have burst with the weight and plunged into the desert hundreds of feet below. Two concentric walls, with a space between, would lighten the pressure and hold the floor.

The pavilion was 65 feet below the Herodian living quarters on the top, summit terrace. The explorers now descended the cliff another 42 feet from the middle terrace to the third, by the remains of a staircase that had once been a covered way to shield the users from the mountain wind—and perhaps Herod's more timorous guests from the sight of the terrifying drop that lay to their left. In 1963 all that remained of this was a broken narrow shelf on the cliff-face open to the sky. Moving along it, the explorers leaned into the cliff lest a sudden gust of wind or a false step pluck them out into

An aerial view of the second tier of Herod's cliff palace. The inner wall was built by Herod's engineers to reduce outward pressure on the perimeter wall.

space and death: any stone their feet dislodged caused a small avalanche hundreds of feet below which trickled out before the sound of its beginning reached up from the depths.

Turning the corner at the bottom of the staircase, the explorers found themselves on a square platform heaped with rubble. Josephus had recorded that this had been a wonderful room with interior walls panelled in marble. As the rubble was cleared away, the panels appeared. And as the sun shone upon them for the first time in nineteen centuries, the expedition saw there was a deception! The panels were imitation marble. Herod had either been unable to obtain real marble or was too thrifty to pay the price marble slabs commanded in his day. So he made his masons smooth the rock-face in oblongs, cover the oblongs with plaster and then paint them dark green, ox-blood red and veined to look like marble. They were crude reproductions—what modern fabricators might call 'instant marble'.

But having been marvellously preserved by the shelter Herod gave them, and then by burial, how were these paintings to survive now that they were suddenly exposed to the abrasive sand-laden winds of the twentieth century? Attempts to inject glue behind them, to keep the plaster attached to the rock, all failed. So experts were called in from Italy who removed the panels, ground away the plaster backing down to a thickness of only one millimetre, and then gave them a new and durable backing. It would have been easier to transport them to the conditioned air of one of the world's great museums, and in the old days this would almost certainly have been done. But in a more enlightened age the expedition felt—and who could disagree?—that no museum could be as fitting as the place where they had given pleasure to their first beholders. So, having been restored, they were put back where Herod's interior decorators had ordered them, and were then covered with transparent plastic panes.

Josephus was mistaken over another feature of this magnificent chamber. He had reported that the pillars in the rear wall of the room were cut out of the solid rock. The expedition proved, however, that the columns were made of separate drums chiselled from soft stone, keyed together and then plastered and fluted to give the appearance of giant monoliths. The masons' marks on each drum were in Hebrew. So Herod's builders had been Jews.

Air photographs of the summit of Masada showed long, narrow strips of rubble behind the northern palace as if some mammoth plough had furrowed a field of rocks. Early explorers had guessed these to be the ruins of ancient barracks. After the great fire, earth-quakes are known to have completed the destruction of these buildings, and since the ridges, when inspected on the ground, were seen to be the foundations of thick walls of stone blocks weighing between 400 lb and 500 lb each, it was supposed that other blocks lying near had been shaken down by earth tremors more or less vertically. So the expedition decided to restore the shattered buildings first and dig into the foundations afterwards. In fact all the dislodged stone blocks were still there and when the last of them had been lifted back into its place it was seen that the original walls had been eleven feet high. Only the original roofs were not recoverable, but they had not been totally destroyed. Charred beams were found three feet down in the ashes of the Masada fire. And now it became clear that the barracks theory was wrong. In the long narrow buildings, each separated by about four feet from the next, the explorers found masses of broken pottery when they reached the floors. Fragments from each room differed from those in the next, and when many vessels had been reassembled by restorers at the base camp it transpired that those from one of the buildings had contained only oil, those in another contained wine, and jars from a third building had held only dried fruit. One jar was marked 'Best dried figs'. Remains of food, apparently deliberately left intact by the Zealots as Josephus had reported, were found there too: walnut shells, pomegranate husks, salt, wheat, and the stones of dates. Wine jars sent from Italy were marked 'To King Herod of Judea'—the first discovery of his name at Masada. The supposed barracks had been his pantries.

When the pantries were almost cleared the diggers came upon a heap of bronze coins and nearly 250 pieces of broken pottery, each bearing a single Hebrew letter or group of letters. Why were they there? Jewish bronze coins from the time of the revolt could have no normal use as money on Masada: there was nothing for the besieged to buy or sell. The archaeologists believed these were related to a system of ration coupons collected by the store keeper.

In the north-west corner of the storerooms complex was a puzzling ruin, believed by earlier travellers to have been a guard house. On excavation there appeared instead a marvellous bathroom, the main hot-room floor supported on two hundred stumpy pillars so that hot air could warm the floor and travel up clay pipes in the walls to vents at various levels. The Romans were great lovers of bathrooms and made a ceremony of going from a dressing room where they left

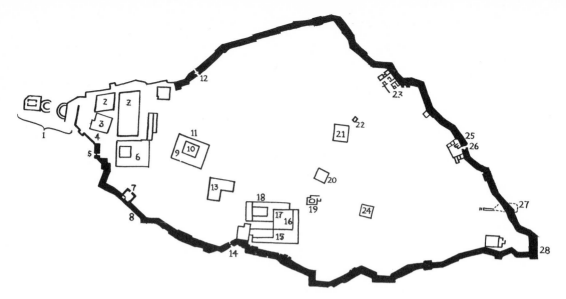

GENERAL PLAN OF MASADA AND THE DISCOVERIES THERE

1 Herod's cliff palace
2 Storerooms
3 The large bath house
4 Spot where the 'lots' were found
5 Water gate
6 Administrative building
7 Synagogue
8 Casemate in which the first scrolls were found
9 Room where a large hoard of silver shekels was found
10 Small Byzantine structure
11 Apartment building
12 Snake-path gate
13 Byzantine church
14 West gate
15 Herod's western palace
16 Throne room
17 Multi-coloured mosaic
18 Service wing
19 Swimming pool
20 Small palace
21 Small palace
22 Byzantine structure with mosaic work-shop
23 Zealots' living quarters
24 Small palace converted into Zealots' quarters
25 Ritual bath
26 Southern water gate
27 Huge underground cistern
28 Southern bastion

their clothes, to the dry hot room, then to the steam chamber, then to the tepidarium to cool off gradually, then to the frigidarium which was usually a deep pool of cold water for a brisk submersion, and back to the dressing room. Herod had provided all this in the unlikeliest place on earth.

On the western edge of the cliffs he built his main palace, with reception halls, throne room and service wing, and on the central plateau three smaller palace villas. Peeling away the deposits of time and decay, the expedition found among these ruins beautiful multi-coloured mosaics. Picks and shovels and even trowels were laid aside when the floors appeared, and the teams took up soft brushes instead and then bulbs like those from old-fashioned motorhorns to blow away the last of the dust without damaging the delicate mosaics. Unsunned for centuries, they now shone in the daylight like brilliant carpets.

But the greatest treasures were still lying under the edges of

Masada's rocky skin: beneath the ruins of the hollow fortifications round the rim of the rock where the Zealots had lived in small rooms, from which they fought, and where in the end, all on one day in April 73 AD, they died.

Nothing of Herod's royal magnificence matched the poignance of these fire-blackened walls, the small heaps of burned cloth and broken clay stoves. And it was here that the expedition reached the goal that Yadin had dreamed of: the finding of written scrolls. There were fragments of the Psalms, the Book of Leviticus containing the list of permissible and forbidden foods that still form the basis of the dietary laws of Orthodox Jewry, and part of Genesis. Here at last were Biblical documents earlier than 73 AD, whose date cannot be disputed.

In all the expedition found fourteen scrolls. Two of them had been carefully concealed beneath the floor of the synagogue the Zealots had built during the siege—the oldest synagogue yet found. These scrolls, hidden in separately dug pits, contained the last two chapters

Herod the Great's casemate walls around the edge of Masada. The Zealots who later occupied the fortress partitioned off these double walls as living and fighting quarters for themselves and their families.

of the Old Testament Book of Deuteronomy and (in the context of Masada) that most dramatic portion from the Book of Ezekiel of the vision of the dry bones: '. . . these bones are the whole house of Israel: behold they say, Our bones are dried up, and our hope is lost . . . thus sayeth the Lord God: Behold I will open up your graves, O my people; and I will bring you into the land of Israel.' Ezekiel, who had been a priest in Jerusalem, was carried away into Babylonian captivity in 597 BC, but prophesied that there would be a great temple of the future and a new Israel risen from the dead.

The texts of both scrolls are almost identical with the Hebrew texts of the Old Testament. Ten of the others were found in the casemate walls, the double fortress walls on the rim of the Masada plateau, partitioned by the Zealots to make living rooms, and among them were sacred writings not included in the Bible we know today. In the third and second century before Christ, Jewish exiles in Alexandria, where Greek was the spoken language, had translated their old scriptures into Greek so that their children would not lose touch with their Jewish faith. But after 70 AD a group of learned rabbis met at Yavne, a seaside place near what is now the city of Tel Aviv, and there selected some sacred writings and discarded others to make our present Old Testament. The discarded writings are called the Apocrypha, which means 'hidden away', and the Pseudepigrapha, which means 'false writing'—that is, not divinely inspired. After these were dropped, they no longer appeared in Hebrew.

The most important book of the Pseudepigrapha was the Book of Jubilees, written in the second half of the second century before Christ. It is a history of the world from the Creation to the time of Moses, and is so called because it divided time into jubilee periods of 49 years each. One of the scrolls turned out to be the Book of Jubilees in its original Hebrew.

One of the most important books in the Apocrypha was Ecclesiasticus, or the Wisdom of Ben Sira. Ben Sira in the second century BC sang the praises of wise and righteous men of ancient Israel, telling of the rewards of studying wisdom as a guide to good conduct. Though the rabbis at Yavne rejected its inclusion in the Old Testament canon, and it ceased to appear in Hebrew, it had been translated into Greek in Alexandria by Ben Sira's grandson towards the end of the second century BC, and passed on to the Christian Church. That is why it is still widely used in the Roman Catholic liturgy today. Portions of this book, too, were contained in another of the scrolls—again in its original and long-lost Hebrew form.

The discovery of the Ecclesiasticus scroll at once settled a dispute among scholars of the world that had lasted for seventy years. For until 1896 the Wisdom of Ben Sira was known only in Greek and Syriac translations. Then in 1896 a forgotten archive was found in a neglected upper room of the Ezra Synagogue in old Cairo which had been founded 1,000 years earlier. Two travelling Scotswomen bought in Cairo some fragments from the synagogue loft and took them back to Cambridge. There one of the fragments was found to be a portion of Ecclesiasticus in Hebrew. The dispute that ensued among scholars was whether this was in the original Hebrew or whether it represented a re-translation from the Greek. The Masada scroll, found in a stratum of undisputed date, was basically identical with the Cairo manuscript, and thus proved it to be in the original Hebrew.

Another scroll found in a room in the walls settled no argument but rather re-kindled controversy that will continue for years to come. Josephus recorded that one way in which the Roman soldiers liked to torment the Jews was to tear up books of the Bible in front of them. This scroll looked as if it had been cut and torn deliberately, but it was not a Bible scroll. It was the Songs of the Sabbath Sacrifices, identical with the text of one of the famous Dead Sea Scrolls found in 1947 in a cave near Qumran, a few miles north of Masada. Most scholars believe that ruins near the caves are those of a headquarters of a Jewish sect called Essenes, formed in the century before Christ. The Essenes were grave and quiet bachelors, wearing long white robes, electing to live a communal life of poverty, practising cere-monial washing akin to baptism, and eating ritual meals with a presiding elder blessing bread and wine. The similarity of all this to Christian practice is startling, but there were also important dif-ferences. The Essenes preached hate for their enemies, and Professor Yadin did not believe they were pacifists. On the contrary he believed, with a majority of scholars, that the Essenes had fought alongside the Zealots in the rebellion that ended at Masada. Josephus, who in his history listed the names of commanders in the revolt, recorded that in the central sector of Palestine, which included what is now Lod airport and Jaffa, the commander was 'John the Essene'. From this, and the finding of an Essene scroll at Masada, Professor Yadin concluded that the Essenes joined the resistance movement at Masada and fought with their fellow Jews till that last April day in 73 AD.

After labouring for a total of eleven months spread over two and a half years, and moving and sifting 50,000 cubic metres of earth,

Vessels restored from fragments found at Masada

the expedition had thrown vivid shafts of new light on life in Palestine in the century of Christ's life. And yet it had been the terrible drama of the last days of Masada that had most fired the imagination of the excavators—the drawing of lots and the mass suicide—and led them to hope they would find confirmation of the tragedy.

In a network of caves near the top of the southern cliff of Masada they found 25 skeletons. Medical examination showed that fourteen were skeletons of men between the ages of 22 and sixty; one was of a man over the age of seventy; six were of females aged between fifteen and 22; four were of children between the ages of eight and twelve; and there were the remains of one embryo. Even more poignant than this collective testimony was a discovery that came when the explorers cleared away rubble at the entrance to a small sunken bathroom at Herod's northern palace. Here lay before them, suddenly, a *précis* of the whole tragic Masada sequence: coins bearing the inscription 'The Freedom of Zion', minted during the revolt when the hope of salvation must have been in its zenith; a letter in Aramaic, the vanished language of Christ's day; fragments of a prayer shawl; hundreds of silver-plated scales of armour; and, last of all, lying on the steps leading down to the pool, the skeletons of a man, a child and a woman, her neatly plaited brown hair still clinging to her scalp, and at her feet her still wearable sandals.

What will for ever remain the most intriguing discovery of the Masada expedition, however, was made on the summit, but its full significance was spotted only by experts at the base camp when they were examining inscribed pieces of pottery brought down in baskets from what had seemed a humdrum day of work. From the systematic numbering of the location of finds, the base camp knew that a group of fragments that seized their interest came from what must have been one of the most strategic spots on the rock at the time of the Roman siege—close to the north-western brink where all the northern tracks on the summit meet. The baskets from this place that came down the wire rope over a period of days brought eleven strange pieces of pottery different from all others found during the exploration. They were inscribed with eleven different names, but all appeared to have been written by the same hand. Could these be the very lots cast to decide who should be the garrison's own executioners? Josephus reported that there were ten lots cast, and here were eleven. The startling thing was that the eleventh bore the name of Ben Ya'ir. And the experts concluded that this could have been no other than Eleazar ben Ya'ir, the leader of the doomed garrison.

The name 'Ben Ya'ir' inscribed on one of the eleven pottery fragments

94

# 6

# The Last Prince

Neither the Jews who were lucky enough to escape slavery after their disastrous revolt of 66–73 AD, nor followers of the new religion of Christianity, were allowed to set foot in the holy ruins of Jerusalem, on pain of death. The Romans, having sacked the city and destroyed the Temple, turned what was left into dreary garrison quarters for the Tenth Legion. The Legion was still there more than fifty years later when Hadrian became Roman Emperor. Hadrian's concern was to make the empire safe. In Asia he gave up the aggressive policies of his predecessor, Trajan, and fixed the River Euphrates as a boundary. He built defensive walls in what is now Germany; and in Britain one can still see the remains of Hadrian's Wall, winding $73\frac{1}{2}$ miles across the narrowest part of England from Wallsend-on-Tyne to Bowness at the head of Solway Firth.

Roman coin of Hadrian

In Jerusalem he established a Roman colony and called it Aelia Capitolina. It was a mistake. At the sight of a foreign pagan settlement spreading over sacred Jewish soil, indignation began to boil up in the Jews who remained, and in 132 AD they rose again in a last bid for freedom. They were led by Shimon bar Kokhba. He proclaimed an independent State and distributed a coinage struck from defaced Roman money. The Romans summoned Julius Severus from his governorship in Britain to crush the insurrection in Palestine, and in three years he was able to report to Rome that the task was complete. The synagogues were destroyed and the defeated Jews followed deported survivors of the First Jewish War into the foreign slave markets. The story of the Israelites had ended.

Shimon bar Kokhba was a lost hero, more myth than man, a shadowy champion whose forlorn defiance the Jews in exile treasured

95

OPPOSITE Painted
panels and carved
columns on the third
and lowest terrace of
Herod's luxurious
hanging palace.

in folk memory, but without knowing where he was born, where he died, or how he died. Indeed it was not known for certain how to spell his name, which means 'son of a star'. He figures only fitfully in later Jewish writings, in the works of the Greek historian Dio Cassius and the Christian Fathers, Eusebius and Jerome.

In 1951 Gerald Lankester Harding of Britain and the French Dominican Father Roland de Vaux, both archaeologists working in Jordan, came into possession of some letters dating from the year 130 AD. They included several copies of a document proclaiming the liberation of the Jews, and described as having come from an unknown source. But archaeologists in the Jewish half of Jerusalem suspected that roaming Bedouin had found the documents in caves in Israeli territory. In 1960 the Israel Exploration Society sent an expedition to explore caves in the neighbourhood of the Dead Sea and find if anything precious remained after the Bedouin plunder. The region is desolate and daunting, split with canyons which are 900 to 1,200 feet deep. The sand-coloured cliffs are pitted with dark spots that are the mouths of caves. Four teams divided the area between them for search and Professor Yigael Yadin led one of them to a strip of territory in which a canyon called Nahal Hever runs down to the Dead Sea near En-gedi.

This is the place where David sought refuge from the murderous jealousy of King Saul, and when Saul was informed that his quarry was 'in the wilderness of En-gedi', the Book of Samuel says he took 3,000 men to seek out and kill David 'upon the rocks of the wild goats'. Saul went into one cave to relieve himself in privacy, the very cave, says the Bible, in whose dark recesses David and his followers were hiding. And stealing forward quietly David snipped a piece from the hem of Saul's robe to signify that though he had an undreamed of opportunity he was unwilling to kill a king he believed to be the Lord's anointed.

The wilderness, the gorges and the caves have not changed in the three thousand years between Saul's search among the caves and the search of the archaeologists for records and remains of Biblical times. But instead of toiling over the rocks of the wild goats, Yadin first organised a reconnaissance by helicopter, taking close-up photographs of the cliff walls whilst the machine hovered like some great hawk over the depths between. The photographs were then pasted on a big board to give a panorama of the whole terrain. Through a magnifying glass Yadin examined every crevice for clues; and on the cliff top above one cave he studied some shapes and shadows

The Roman siege camp on the cliff above the Cave of Letters in Nahal Hever.

Seventeen bronze Roman cult vessels found in the first hall of the Cave of Letters at Nahal Hever.

which he recognised as the remains of a Roman camp. Clearly the neighbourhood and its people must at one time have warranted stationing a military force in this unusual place, and the nearest caves—especially the one immediately beneath the ruins—became a target for immediate investigation.

From their desert base camp Yadin's party travelled by truck over the stony landscape to the cliff tops and looked over the edge. There seemed to be no simple way to reach the cave. They could see a narrow and perilous path, only twelve inches wide, leading over the precipice obliquely—the sort of path a wild goat might use— but it went down to a point fifty feet below the cave entrance and to a ledge hanging over the void. Furthermore, they could see there was a gap in the ledge. If they used the path the gap in the ledge would have to be crossed, and here one part of the track had eroded and sloped away from the cliff face. But there was no alternative, and so, slowly and carefully, they made their way down the path, leaning towards the rock wall as they went, knowing that turning dizzy could lead to a false step and that any first false step could be the last. They reached the ledge and stopped to consider what to do next. One member of the team volunteered to try to climb up to the cave. He was taking his life in his hands. Discarding his boots in order to use his toes to get a better purchase, he edged his way up the vertical

97

Crossing the gap in
the perilous descent
to the Cave of Letters.

rock face, looking, from the canyon floor a thousand feet below,
like a fly crawling up a wall. At last the anxious watchers saw him
reach his objective, and there in the cave mouth he hitched the top
of a rope ladder securely to a rock. One by one the others then climbed
the ladder.

At the cave mouth they were at the start of a low-roofed corridor
which descended into the cliff for about twenty-five feet and ended
at a barrier of stones. They could see the cave continued beyond the
blockage, and when they had made their way over it they found
themselves in a chamber the size of a biggish house. From this
chamber the team entered a winding passage which led into a second
chamber as big as the first, and this, in turn gave access to a third
chamber. Here, in the ancient dark, breathing became difficult:
not only because of the depth—about four hundred and fifty feet
from the cave entrance and daylight—but also because it was infested
with thousands of bats, and the stench from them and from their
accumulated dung was almost unbearable. Another horror awaited
them. When Yadin squeezed through the opening into the third
chamber and shone his torch into a long niche opening off it, its
beam lighted up a scene to startle the most hardened explorer.
One wall of this part of the cave was lined with baskets, and every
basket was overflowing with human skulls. He was in a burial
chamber. Layer upon layer of mats covered human bones. Between

the mats and bones were fragments of coloured cloth wonderfully well preserved in the dry air. Baskets made of woven palm leaves looked as if they might have been put there only last year instead of centuries ago.

Who were these people? How had they met their deaths? From famine and thirst with Roman soldiery pinning them down in their cave from above? And who had filled the baskets, laid out the bones and mats, and been the last to die? There was no answer yet. But several days later a student in the group found a small coin in the dust. On one side was a palm tree and the inscription 'Shimon'. On the other side was a bunch of grapes, and the words *Leherut Yerushalayim*—'of the freedom of Jerusalem'. Yadin was now convinced that they were on the track of Bar Kokhba, and that the skeletons were those of fighters in his rebellion.

Using a mine detector, and starting from the place where the coin was found, the team worked through all the chambers. For a long time this produced nothing. Then, about thirty feet from the entrance to the first chamber, the mine detector began to buzz, its needle flicking. Since there were no signs of metal to be seen, the team thought the reaction might be caused by their own work-tools. These were cleared away. Still the detector buzzed. They sent away all the men with nails in their boots. The detector buzzed on. So they began to dig in the stones and rubble. What first came to light was a basket like those that had been packed with skulls, its handles tied with rope. Yadin untied the knot and put his hand inside. He brought out a copper jug so well preserved it looked as if it had left

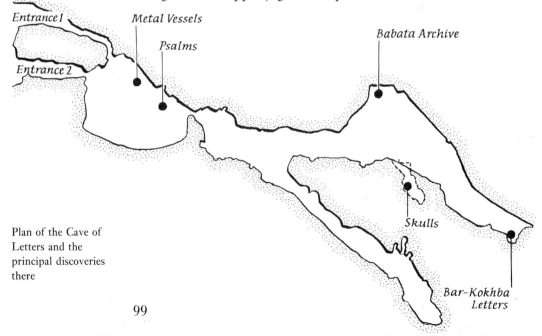

Plan of the Cave of Letters and the principal discoveries there

Working in the Cave. Lack of oxygen stifled the pneumatic drills, which had to be abandoned.

the craftsman's hands in our own times. Then out came more metal jugs large and small, twelve of them, some engraved near the handles with heads of birds and palm leaf motifs. The basket also yielded three incense shovels, a shallow ritual vessel of fine workmanship, and a five-pronged key. In the bottom of the basket were two large bowls, to the handle of one of which was attached the other end of the rope that tied the basket's handles: it was a neat piece of packing. Some of the figures of Roman deities stamped on the handles of vessels appeared to have been rubbed out deliberately, but it was clear that here were original Roman cult vessels for sacrifices and libations to the gods. What Yadin and his men had unearthed was probably booty taken by Bar Kokhba's fighters from some Roman camp before they themselves were forced to flee to the cave.

Immensely excited now, the explorers asked the Army for more help, and Israel's Engineering Corps brought an electric generator to the top of the cliff and flooded the caves with light. This brought a dramatic turn to the search. Only one hour after work had resumed under electric light one of the workers found a fragment of scroll made of leather. There was Hebrew writing on it. Hebrew is a language whose script has changed scarcely at all over the centuries, and since this writing was very clear they could read it immediately: '*Yagur be'chlekha . . .*' and then, '*Tamin ufo'el tzedek . . .*' It was Psalm 15 —'Lord, who shall abide in thy tabernacle? Who shall dwell in Thy holy hill?' But the greatest find was yet to come.

That same afternoon, in the innermost chamber where there was a crevice between the wall and some large rocks, a member of the team named Yoram found a water skin of goathide. There was something inside it, but being unable to lift the skin out bodily, he began feeling in it and handing out its contents to his colleagues: bundles of raw wool wrapped in cloth and skeins of wool in many colours; strings of beads, a bone spoon, metal beads and a spindle, packages containing salt, a peppercorn, sea shells—some woman's treasured possessions. Then Yoram passed up a small package tied with cord. It was a collection of papyri, and between the papyri were slats of thin wood bearing written inscriptions. The team put these in a box lined with cotton wool and took it to Jerusalem. There were four wooden slats and at the end of one was cursive writing in ink. Yadin knew already he had made a priceless discovery, but even he could scarcely believe what he then saw.

Wooden powder box and glass cosmetic oil container from the goatskin water bottle

The writing said: *Shimon bar Kosebah hannasi al Yisrael— Shimon bar Kokhba, Prince over Israel.* Still unable to believe it, Yadin went straight to see Professor Nahman Avigad, one of the world's experts on Hebrew epigraphy, and drew the letters for him. Avigad studied the writing for several minutes and then looked up with a sparkle of joy in his eyes. The two men embraced without speaking. They had in their possession the first discovery in Israel of inscriptions on wood dating back to within a hundred years of Christ.

As for the rest of the inscriptions, they were as thrilling to Jews as discoveries of military instructions from the legendary King Arthur at Camelot would be to anybody in Britain. There was an order from Bar Kokhba addressed to two men called Jonathan and Masabala, instructing them to confiscate wheat belonging to Tahnun bar Yishmael and to send it to him under guard; Bar Kokhba threatened punishment for disobedience. Another message revealed Bar Kokhba commanding the same men, Jonathan and Masabala, to harvest within the areas under their command and send the wheat to the camp. So it seems that Jonathan and Masabala ruled an area of cultivated land at a time when Bar Kokhba was still commanding

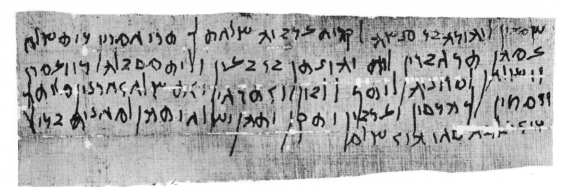

Letter in Aramaic in which Bar Kokhba asks for ritual supplies for celebrating the Feast of Tabernacles.

forces against the Romans; and one or both of them had brought the letters with them when they took refuge in the cave. The writing was in Aramaic; but then came a letter in Hebrew which revealed where Jonathan and Masabala lived. It began, 'From Shimon bar Kokhba to the men of En-gedi, to Masabala and Yehonaltan bar Be'ayan: Greeting!'

Another letter placed another resistance group at Teqoah, eleven miles south of Jerusalem on the edge of the desert, an important military and agricultural centre mentioned in the Bible—it is recorded in the Book of Nehemiah that the nobles of Teqoah refused to contribute their share to the reconstruction of the ramparts of Jerusalem. Since Jonathan and Masabala were required by Bar Kokhba, under threat of punishment, to send the people of Teqoah to him, the conclusion is that the area controlled by Jonathan and Masabala included this city, and extended at least from En-gedi on the east to Teqoah in the west and comprised the central sector of Judean desert and the coast of the Dead Sea. En-gedi was clearly an important supply centre for Bar Kokhba's men. It was rich in farmland (it is still an oasis) and had a harbour on the western shores of the Dead Sea. The cave of Nahal Hever is only three and a half miles from En-gedi. It would be natural for the fighters in this region who were alive and at liberty when the revolt crumbled, to seek refuge in canyon caves in the Judean desert, and for each to choose the nearest caves when it became obvious that further resistance was useless. En-gedi's men came to Nahal Hever.

Brass mirror in wooden case found near the Bar Kokhba letters

Another letter, adding flesh and human foible to the ghost-hero, showed that Bar Kokhba was not always satisfied with the service of Jonathan and Masabala. The Prince complains: 'You sit and eat and drink of the property of the House of Israel and care nothing for your brothers.'

One further letter excited the Israelis. It was addressed by Bar

Kokhba, not to Jonathan and Masabala, but to Yehuda bar Menashe, at Oiryat 'Arabaya, and informed him: 'I have sent you two donkeys so that you may send two men with them to Jonathan bar Be'ayan and Masabala to load them with palm branches and citrons and send them back to your camp. You, on your part, send others to bring you willows and myrtle . . . and send them to the camp.' Oiryat 'Arabaya does not persist in any modern place name, but it could possibly be identified with Birath 'Arava, Bethlehem. Almost certainly the letter was written about preparations for the Feast of the Tabernacles, a harvest festival which also commemorates the wandering of the Jews, and in order to supply the soldiers at Bar Kokhba's camp with the required four kinds of plants for the feast.

Yadin's expedition ceased its work as the hot summer days approached, but in the following March, in 1961, a second expedition set out from Jerusalem for the Judean desert, with young Israeli and foreign volunteers to renew the search. Yadin took one team to what was now known as the Cave of Letters. And there they found what had escaped them in the previous year—a basket containing women's sandals, and farming and household utensils, and 35 more documents. Out of the contents of the basket and the unrolled papyri emerged, fragment by fragment, a mosaic of life and laws and customs in the hundred years in Palestine after Christ. It showed that land under Bar Kokhba's control was nationalised in his name as head of the rebel Jewish State. As Prince of Israel he assumed the rights of the Roman Emperor. His rule was tightly organised. His civil servants in towns and villages had charge of local affairs, supervising the leasing of land to tenant farmers and collecting taxes from them. The farmers grew dates and grain and harvested wheat with sickles like those still used by Arab peasants. The women wore sandals very like those Israeli women favour today and called Elath sandals—after the resort on the Gulf of Elath in the south. Men and women ate off wooden plates, and washed or licked them clean after use: those found in the cave were spotless and the knives with them were still sharp.

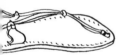

Woman's sandal found with Babata's archive

Among the contents of the basket was an archive of 35 deeds and contracts, the biggest single collection of ancient documents of this kind ever found in the Holy Land. Six of them were written in the language of the Nabateans, a Semitic people of Arab stock whose city of Petra in southern Jordan is celebrated for its red rock tombs, and whose writing was, until recent times, known only in inscriptions cut into this rock. These documents covered a period of twelve years

in the life of the owner of the archive, a woman hitherto unknown
to history. Deeds and contracts are dull-sounding things, but to the
scholars who opened them it was like opening a door into a society
centuries in advance of our western way of life at that time, and re-
vealing the habits and customs of the well-to-do people Jesus knew.

This is the story the documents told:

In the year 120 AD there lived in the village of Mahoza in the
district of Zoar, a farmer named Shimeon, the son of Menahem.
Zoar is at the southern tip of the Dead Sea and the Book of Genesis
tells us that Zoar is where Lot, the nephew of Abraham, found refuge when God brought destruction to the evil cities of Sodom
and Gomorrah. Shimeon farmed date groves. He had water rights
clearly specified for each tract of land: 'half an hour from the stream
on Sundays . . . Wednesdays one hour . . .' Water was precious.

Shimeon was a prudent, prosperous and thoughtful family man.
He looked ahead. On July 14 in that year he gave all his property—
houses, courtyards, gardens and groves—to his wife Miriam. It was
all to be hers for life. But there were conditions. Shimeon reserved
the right to any debts due to him and to live in his own house. Miriam
must continue to perform all the duties of a faithful wife 'until the
day when I go to my last resting place'.

Shimeon and Miriam had a daughter named Babata. She was
married to a man named Joshua, the son of Joseph. Perhaps Joshua
was not a very sturdy man, or Shimeon suspected this; for he stipulat-
ed in the deed of gift to his wife that if Babata became a widow
whilst her mother was still alive, she could have the use of one of
her father's storehouses for as long as she remained a widow. The
archive was Babata's. It seems she hoarded documents as a squirrel
hoards nuts, and the rest of the papers are like snapshots of her
troubled life. It turned out that her husband Joshua was indeed a
doomed man. He died less than four years later, for another deed in
the archive, dated 124 AD, reveals that at a council meeting at Petra
two guardians were appointed for Babata's orphaned son, Joshua
junior. This was the beginning of a whole string of disputes. On
October 12 in the year 125 AD Babata filed a claim with the Roman
provincial governor for the payment of money owed to her son by
his guardians. She had married again and taken as her second husband
Yehuda, a son of Eleazar, a man from En-gedi who had come to live
in Mahoza. Babata's marriage certificate was there among the
documents, but the exact date had decayed. At any rate, whether
married to Babata or still only a suitor, Yehuda in October 125 AD

Professor Yadin and his team recording the contents of the palm-leaf basket in which was found the archive of Babata.

was representing her in her claim to the Roman governor.

Yehuda had been on good terms with the local Roman garrison—good enough terms with some of them anyway, to be able as an impoverished bachelor to borrow sixty Tyrian silver dinars from Valens, who was Centurion of the First Thracian Cohort of a Thousand Infantry. For in May 124 AD he had promised to repay the loan plus twelve per cent interest, or as the deed says, 'I shall pay you monthly the rate of one denarius in one hundred denarii . . .' over the following eight months. As security, with or without parental knowledge, Yehuda pledged as collateral 'the compound belonging to my father Eleazar', the boundaries of which were 'to the east, tents . . . to the west, tents and workshops of that same Eleazar, my father; south, the market . . . and north, the road and fort.'

So at that time there was a company of one hundred Thracian auxiliaries encamped at En-gedi. The presence here in the Judean desert of the cohort to which the unit of auxiliaries was attached was unknown until this document was found. The site of Eleazar's workshop and the compound Yehuda put in pawn can easily be visualised, close to the Roman soldiers and the fort, and perhaps even servicing them. From this and other documents, indeed, it was possible for the archaeologists to draw a map of En-gedi as perhaps Jesus and John the Baptist knew it—its lands, its buildings, markets and citadels in detail. This is the archaeologist's ultimate reward.

But to return to Babata. Before the year 125 AD was out she was certainly Yehuda's wife and she sought trusteeship of her son Joshua's money held by his guardians, promising to pay a higher rate of interest than the guardians and to mortgage her property. If her petition is granted, she swears to the colonial power, her son will live 'thankfully praising the happy days of the hegemony' of the governor. We may guess that this patently insincere phrase was an expected, but purely formal piece of flattery which deceived nobody, least of all a Roman ruler. Her request was granted, and she kept the proof of it, written in Greek and signed by Yehuda on her behalf, because Babata could not write Greek. Seven witnesses signed it, too.

The next two years seem to have passed more quietly for Babata. She was looking after her property and her son's interests and managing Yehuda's household. In the winter of 127 AD she travelled with him to the headquarters of the Roman cavalry unit in Rabbath-Moab, the capital of Moab, to declare her property to the Roman district officer, Priscus, for a land census taken that year by the Roman governor of Provincia Arabia. This was the province established by the Emperor Trajan in 106 AD in place of the last vassal kingdom in Palestine, which was Nabatea with its capital at Petra. Babata's property was measured by the amount of wheat required to sow it and the expected produce of her date groves. She had five acres of date palms.

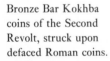

Bronze Bar Kokhba coins of the Second Revolt, struck upon defaced Roman coins.

Professor G. Bieberkraut begins to unroll the archive of Babata. He also unrolled the first of the Dead Sea Scrolls to be acquired by Israel in 1948.

Then Yehuda died, leaving Babata a lot more property—and trouble with it. For Yehuda's relatives claimed that this property belonged mainly to his father Eleazar. And the next documents revealed a further family complication: evidently before Yehuda married Babata he had already been wedded to another girl from En-gedi called Miriam, and by this first wife Yehuda seems to have had a daughter called Shelamzion. Her name means 'Peace of Zion'. When her father died she, too, came into a slice of his En-gedi property. We do not know when Yehuda died, except that it was before the autumn of 130 AD; for in September of that year Babata leased part of her date groves in Mahoza to a local Jew, perhaps because she could no longer manage them single-handed or afford hired labour; for her new tenant acknowledges that he has received fruit from 'the date groves of Yehuda, your late husband . . . which, according to your claim, you received in exchange for your bride price and the debt he owed you.' The local man agrees to pay Babata 42 talents of the best quality dates, and some of second quality which are to be weighed in her house 'on Mahoza scales'. Then he can keep the rest of the crop for his labour and expenses. A second document sets out Babata's obligation to her contractor if she does not meet her side of the bargain.

Two months after making this deal—in November 130 AD—the guardians of Joseph junior accuse her of keeping a date grove which her second husband Yehuda signed over to her illegally. The lawsuit lasts until July 131, with the disputants hurling charges and counter-charges at each other. Babata got herself a Nabatean lawyer from Petra to fight her case. Perhaps it was on his advice that she not only refutes the guardians' charges but, using legal tactics that have become familiar down the ages, goes over to the attack, accusing the guardians of slandering her before the Roman governor. What the upshot was we shall, alas, never know: for at this point the papyrus had so decayed that it cannot be read further.

But other troubles were building up to plague the life of twice-widowed Babata. In 131 she tells the provincial governor Haterius Nepos that Miriam of En-gedi has stolen 'property from the house of Yehuda . . . your husband and my husband.' Babata was now quarrelling with her second husband's other wife, and Miriam raps back through her lawyer, 'I have warned you before to keep your hands off Yehuda's goods.' What judgment Haterius Nepos handed down is unknown to us: if it was recorded Babata did not keep this particular document. More significant, however, than this, is the fact that the document recording the quarrel between the two women explains how Babata and her family reached the Cave of Letters after the start of the revolt of the Jews against their Roman masters began in 132 AD. For in the summons taken out by Babata to bring Miriam to court over Yehuda's estate, Miriam's full name is given as 'Miriam, daughter of Be'ayan of En-gedi'. In other words she was the sister of Jonathan, son of Be'ayan—the Jonathan who, with Masabala, ruled En-gedi on behalf of Bar Kokhba during the revolt. When Jonathan fled to the Cave of Letters as the revolt began to fail, he brought along with him not only his immediate family, but other relatives too. And among them came Babata, bringing with her the archive that has enabled archaeologists to eavesdrop on the private problems of family life in Palestine in the century after Christ.

The last document is dated 19 August 132 AD, the year of the outbreak of the revolt. It is a receipt from Babata for the guardians of young Joshua for money supplied by them to provide food and clothing. Was it never delivered? There is no answer from the dust. Nor shall we ever know if Miriam, as a relative, was also there; and whether, in the darkening days of their lives the two widows patched up their trivial quarrel before they died of starvation in the beleaguered cave.

# 7

# The Dead Sea Scrolls

Qumran is a parched slope of gravel on the north-western shores of the Dead Sea. It is a place with a quality of stillness impossible to find in the peopled parts of the world. Nobody lives there now, and in the quivering impact of hot air and stony land nothing moves on the ground or in the sky. Behind the slope rise limestone cliffs that have been crumbling for centuries until they look like the earth's scorched and rotten bones. Here, in the spring of 1947, wandered a Bedouin tribe. One of them, a boy called Mohammed the Wolf, who was looking for a goat that had strayed, threw a stone into the mouth of a cave. No goat emerged, but the stone made a small, unusual sound, as of breaking earthenware. The young goatherd was startled and ran away, returning only when another youngster in the tribe came with him.

Inside the cave they found eight jars, five on one side and three on the other, all about two feet tall and with lids like upturned dishes. When they lifted the lids they saw the jars contained long objects, some wrapped in linen. Stripping off some of the cloth, they came upon rolls of leather covered with writing. They could not read it. It was Hebrew, older than the lifetime of Christ and 1,000 years older than the most ancient Biblical Hebrew manuscript then known. The goatherd had stumbled on a discovery that was going to astonish the scholarly world and startle the theological world as no other discovery has ever done.

The Bedouin took the scrolls along with them to Bethlehem, perhaps hoping to dispose of them to some curio hunter and thereby add a little profit to that earned from selling their goats. They used two of the jars from the cave for carrying water. But in Bethlehem

A scroll jar inside a cave near the Dead Sea.

they found it easier to sell goats than the dull bundles from the jars. Nobody wanted them until by chance their existence became known to the head of the Syriac monastery of St Mark, the Metropolitan Samuel, in the Old City of Jerusalem. He was mildly interested, but by the time he decided to make an offer for them the Bedouin had gone off on their wandering again, taking the scrolls with them. Some time later, however, they returned, and the Metropolitan bought five scrolls, for, it is said, £10 each.

Scholars to whom he showed his speculative purchase were unimpressed. Some said they could not be very old; one declared they were not worth a shilling; a third said he didn't believe they had been found in a cave near the Dead Sea—more likely they had been stolen from a Jewish synagogue and the Metropolitan had been duped by wily Arab thieves. The prelate was depressed. In Jerusalem, however, a parallel event was soon to unfold.

On November 23 that year Professor E. L. Sukenik, the archaeologist at the Hebrew University in Jerusalem, received a mysterious message in a telephone call from an excited Armenian antique dealer in the city. The Armenian said he could not explain his purpose on the telephone and asked the professor to meet him.

It was a time of turmoil and tension in Palestine. The British had

ruled the land for thirty years as trustees, first for the League of
Nations and then for the United Nations. But they had been quite
unable to bring Arabs and Jews into an agreement to live peacefully
together, and were about to throw in their hand, quit the country,
and leave both peoples to settle their differences on their own.
Six thousand miles away in the United States the United Nations
were about to vote for the establishment of a sovereign Jewish State,
creating it at what the Arabs saw as their expense. As a means of
keeping control in the meantime, the British had divided Jerusalem
into military zones, marked off with barbed wire barriers guarded
by sentries, and movement of civilians between zones was allowed
only to those with permits. Neither Sukenik nor the Armenian possessed a permit, so they arranged to meet the next morning at a gate-
way between their two zones. There at the barrier the Armenian
took from his briefcase a scrap of leather, and the professor could see
that it was covered with Hebrew script. Where had it come from?
The Armenian said a mutual friend, an Arab antique dealer in
Bethlehem, told him Bedouin had brought the documents to him
saying they had found them near the Dead Sea, not far from Jericho.
The Bedouin had offered to sell the scrolls but the Arab dealer didn't
know whether they were genuine and had asked the Armenian's
advice. He didn't know either, and so he had sought the help of the
professor.

Sukenik, trembling with excitement over what he had seen,
decided to ask for a military permit and travel with the Armenian
to Bethlehem—a hazardous journey because on the very day he
had chosen, November 29, the United Nations vote would declare
part of Palestine to be the new State of Israel, and Jewish joy at the
prospect was overlaid with the foreboding that the Arabs would
make immediate war upon them. And they were right. To forestall
what he saw coming the professor set out early, while it was still
the middle of the night in America. He was the only Jew in a busload
of Arabs and the tension was frightening. Reaching Bethlehem
unhurt, he and the Armenian made their way to the house of the
Arab antique dealer and were invited up to the attic. The professor
described the scene in his diary:

'He (the antique dealer) then brought out two jars in which the
bundles had been found, which he offered for our inspection.
They were of a shape unfamiliar to me. He then carefully produced
the leather scrolls. My hands shook as I started to unroll one of

them. I read a few sentences. It was written in beautiful Biblical Hebrew. The language was like that of the Psalms, but the text was unknown to me. I looked and looked, and I suddenly had the feeling that I was privileged by destiny to gaze upon a Hebrew scroll which had not been read for more than two thousand years . . .'

Sukenik took home with him on approval three scrolls, carrying them in the bus (he recalled) as if they were a parcel of vegetables from market. They turned out to be a scroll of the Book of the Prophet Isaiah, a thanksgiving scroll of 35 hitherto unknown psalms, and an apocalyptic work by an unknown author, telling a dramatic story of how a final war would be fought at the end of time between the Sons of Light and the Sons of Darkness. He sent a message to the Arab dealer that he would buy the scrolls.

A few days after the professor had examined the scrolls he was on his way to lecture when he encountered a friend and told him his exciting news. To his astonishment the friend then revealed that some months earlier (when Sukenik was on a trip to America) the President of the Hebrew University had sent two members of his library staff to the Syriac monastery of St Mark to look at some manuscripts held by the Metropolitan Samuel. The Metropolitan had asked their opinion of the age of the manuscripts and whether the University would buy them. But nothing had come of this. The professor felt certain these scrolls also had come from the Bedouin, but he could not confirm it. And by this time the entrance to the Old City was blocked by the Arabs and he could not visit the monastery. Not until January 1948 did the chance recur. Then the professor received a letter from a Syrian friend inviting him to go to the YMCA building in Zone B of Jerusalem and look at some ancient manuscripts which he and the Syrian Metropolitan had bought from the same Bedouin tribe who had brought the other three scrolls to the Arab antique dealer in Bethlehem. The professor saw at once that these were indeed more Dead Sea scrolls and he offered to buy them, though he had little money and dared not name a price. The deal was deferred to a later meeting. The meeting never took place. Instead, weeks later, the Syrians wrote to say they had decided not to sell until they could discover a proper market price. What had really happened was that the Metropolitan Samuel, still trying to prove his suspicion that the scrolls he possessed, but could not read, were immensely valuable, had at last contacted American scholars. One of them,

The Wadi Qumran, with the ruins of the Essene monastery in the middle distance and the Dead Sea beyond.

having seen a photograph of only part of one of the Metropolitan's scrolls, recognised it as being the Book of Isaiah, and declared that the original must be an 'absolutely incredible find ... the greatest manuscript discovery of modern times.'

But Palestine was about to become a battlefield. Troops from six Arab countries went to war against Israel, and when the fighting developed it prevented scholars from going to the caves in the south. The Syrian Metropolitan, whose monastery was caught in the cross-fire of Arab and Jewish forces, left Jerusalem, taking the scrolls with him. He travelled to other and safer parts of the Middle East, but eventually crossed the Atlantic and arrived in the United States. He stowed the scrolls in a bank safe deposit. Here he thought the leathers would be safe, and perhaps in time he might be able to raise money for his church by selling them to some learned institution or university.

But in the rich New World there seemed to be no eager seekers of antique writing, and he began to despair. Six years had gone by since the war in Palestine. It was now 1954. At last the Metropolitan decided to make one more effort and he put a small advertisement in a newspaper saying he had ancient scrolls to dispose of. It brought no rush of bidders, but it did catch the eye of a Jewish journalist who, having read it, reached for his telephone. Professor Sukenik had died in 1953, believing (as he had noted sadly in his diary) that through the Syrians 'the Jewish people have lost a precious heritage'. But in 1954 the professor's son, Yigael Yadin, was on a lecture tour of the United States and had reached New York. It was to him that the journalist telephoned to ask if he happened to have seen, under the heading of Miscellaneous For Sale, an item on Page 14 of that day's issue of *The Wall Street Journal*. It read:

> Biblical Manuscripts dating back to at least
> 200 BC are for sale. This would be an ideal
> gift to an educational or religious institution by
> an individual or group.
> Box F.206 *The Wall Street Journal*.

Yadin hadn't seen it, but the journalist brought him the paper. It put the professor in a fever of excitement, but also in a quandary. As a widely-known and famous Jew he dared not disclose his interest to the Syrians lest the price asked should rocket, and lest the Arab States (who had already denounced the Metropolitan as a smuggler) should intervene diplomatically to stop any attempt to purchase for Israel scrolls which they believed had been discovered in Arab territory. So Yadin decided to act secretly through an intermediary and a bank. The price was high anyway—after hard haggling the Metropolitan was holding out for a quarter of a million dollars. This was but a fraction of what Yadin guessed the scrolls ought to fetch in an open market, but it was far beyond his own purse. So he cabled his government and waited. His suspense ended when the answer came, 'Buy'. And so Israel acquired four more scrolls and now had seven in all. These were, however, but a fraction of the number coming to light in the Judean desert.

When the Arab-Israeli war of 1948 was over, the cease-fire left Qumran in Jordanian territory and scholars from the French Ecole Biblique and the Jordanian Department of Antiquities hurried south, hoping to find more scrolls. They found, to their dismay, enough broken jars in one cave alone to estimate that at one time it must have held two hundred scrolls. But the scrolls were all gone. Someone had got there first. The Bedouin, having quickly realised what a commotion their first discovery had aroused, had been foraging in other caves, and towards the end of 1951 they had turned up at the Ecole Biblique with handfuls of crumbling papyrus and parchment.

Father Roland de Vaux of the Ecole Biblique and Mr G. Lankester Harding of the Department of Antiquities in Jordan, set out once again for the southern desert, this time with an armed escort. They were afraid that the loot-hungry Bedouin would tear up priceless documents to sell the pieces and so scatter them irretrievably. Their alarm was justified, for when they reached the desert they found the caves infested with searching Arabs. Gangs of them had sentries posted on the hills to flash signals across the wilderness so that they could disappear for a while into clefts in the crags if they were warned of the approach of police or soldiery.

The French monk and the English archaeologist decided to examine as many caves as they could find, and in fact they searched 267. Many were empty, but the two men eventually recovered thousands of scroll fragments, some so fragile that they could turn into dust at the touch of a finger. They knew now that what they had come upon were sections of a dispersed ancient library—a library which examination of the fragments showed included almost all the known books of the Bible, and much else—especially, and most excitingly, the laws, liturgies, prayers, blessings and wisdom of a mysterious Jewish religious sect.

From one cave in 1952 emerged two rolls of sheet copper, so oxidised that they could not be opened on the spot. Instead they were sent to England and at Manchester College of Technology a delicate machine was invented and built to saw the layers of copper into strips. These showed twelve columns of Hebrew writing tapped into the metal. The writing listed a fantastic amount of hidden treasure to which the scrolls purported to be a guide. One early speculation was that here was an inventory of the sacred gold and silver from the Herodian Temple in Jerusalem, taken away and concealed by pious Jews before the Temple was destroyed by the Romans in 70 AD, the record then having been given to the desert sect for safe-keeping. But the historian Josephus had reported that the Temple treasures were burned or stolen by the Romans, and in Rome today, on the Arch of Titus, you may see a relief carving of Titus's troops carrying off Temple spoil. Some treasure may have been salvaged in time and then hidden, but the fabulous amounts listed in the copper scrolls, together with the vague nature of the directions for finding it, led to the belief that the list was more an exercise in folklore than in fact. By 1972 no specified items had been found.

All these discoveries, however, had lent new significance to a

The late Professor H. Wright Baker cutting one of the copper scrolls at the Manchester College of Technology.

Reconstruction of desks from the writing room, the scriptorium, at Qumran

group of hitherto neglected ruins on the shores of the Dead Sea. These could now be seen as a central point geographically among the caves in which scrolls had been found. An early traveller in these desolate regions thought the ruins might be the remains of the Biblical wicked city of Gomorrah. Others thought they were part of a Roman fort. It turned out to be the community centre of the scrolls sect. Excavations soon showed that it was probably occupied in the century between 135 and 37 BC, abandoned during the reign of Herod the Great from 37 to 4 BC, but then re-occupied by the religious sect throughout the years of the ministry of Jesus and until the first Jewish Revolt in 66 AD. The 'monastery' was found to have had between twenty and thirty rooms. There were thirteen water cisterns, chambers which have since been identified as kitchens, storerooms and stables. There was a communal dining-room and a pantry in which lay broken plates, bowls, serving dishes, water and wine flasks—the tableware of the community. There was also a room where the excavators found inkwells, and even traces of ink, and where it is now supposed scribes copied the scrolls. Between the ruins and the edge of the Dead Sea were more than a thousand graves. The evidence was strong that here were the headquarters of a sect that could be named the Essenes.

The Essenes were not unknown before the scroll discoveries. They were a group of austere and dedicated Jews who broke away from the two main branches of their religious authority, the Pharisees and Sadducees. They believed the ruling priesthood in Jerusalem was not legitimate, and that they themselves would one day return to the Temple and restore the purity of Old Testament doctrine. The Roman naturalist Pliny wrote of them as a solitary people 'and extraordinary above all others in the world'. From his writings and those of Josephus and the Alexandrian Jewish philosopher Philo we already knew that these Essenes numbered about 4,000 in Palestine and flourished in the century before Jesus and during his life time. They renounced all wordly pleasure and luxury, wore their clothes and shoes to shreds, owned nothing as individuals, used no money, and—as we now know from the scrolls—looked up to a shadowy Teacher of Righteousness who was their founder. At mealtimes they went to their dining-room in solemn silence and ate nothing until the bread and wine had been blessed by a presiding elder.

The scrolls added immensely to modern knowledge of the Essenes, but one scroll kept its secret for a further seven years after its existence became known. On leave in England in 1961, Professor Yadin was unexpectedly approached by a man claiming to be acting for an antique dealer in Jordan who was offering a scroll for sale. He wanted something like £600,000 for it. For proof of the scroll's possession the agent produced from his pocket tiny fragments stuck together with a British postage stamp: enough, however, to convince Yadin that it could be part of a treasure of incalculable value. He offered the agent less than one-tenth of the sum demanded, and a deal seemed possible when, suddenly and inexplicably, the agent vanished. All efforts to find him or the scroll were fruitless. Not until Israeli forces occupied the Arab sector of Jerusalem in the Six Day War of June 1967 was the dealer tracked down. At first he denied any knowledge of the scroll, but eventually it was found wrapped in a plastic bag and hidden in an old box. A purchase price in the region of Yadin's offer was negotiated, but it soon became obvious why the disappearing agent had named such a vast initial sum. For the scroll was 8·6 metres long—the longest Dead Sea scroll thus far found.

Damp had so accelerated the slow decay of two thousand years that one end of the scroll had turned into a dark brown stump like caked chocolate. It required months of patient skill to unroll it. At one stage it was moistened and then put into a refrigerator so that the sudden drop in temperature congealed the inscribed surface whilst leaving the membrane pliable enough to move. Some un-detachable parts could be read only with the help of infra-red, ultra-violet and X-ray photography. In other parts the ink script had peeled off and stuck in negative form to the back of the layer under-neath: as when one puts a carbon sheet wrong side round in a type-writer. This difficulty was overcome by photographing the back of the scroll and then printing it in reverse.

A potsherd from Qumran, with a scribe's experimental alphabet written on it, and an inkwell from the scriptorium

The scroll's 66 columns of writing contained religious rules ex-tending and varying those in the Bible; a guide to festival sacrifices; architectural notes on how the Temple in Jerusalem ought to be built; and military statutes for a King of Israel and his army.

In all matters of ritual cleanliness the rules in the scroll are stricter than orthodox Jewish law in matters of even ordinary hygiene. They specify, for example, that public lavatories in Jerusalem should be no nearer than 1,370 metres to the Temple and north-west of it for reasons that can be seen to be good today. West of the Temple was undesirable because of prevailing westerly winds; the east was undesirable because this would have meant building the lavatories on the holy Mount of Olives; due north and due south were un-suitable for topographical reasons. Only to the north-west would they be out of scent and sight of the Temple and on lower ground—which is what the scroll prescribes.

For the proper Temple building there are precise measurements for chambers and courtyards, and for twelve gateways named after the twelve tribes. The Essenes considered the Temple built by Herod to be of impure design and not in accord with the wishes of God.

The military statutes stipulate that a bodyguard of 12,000 men—one thousand from each tribe, and 'men of truth, God-fearing, hating unjust gain'—should protect the king day and night. Instructions are given on exactly how the army should react to different degrees of danger. If an enemy comes threatening to 'take everything which belongs to Israel', one-tenth of the army's strength should be mobilised; one-third if the enemy appears 'with his king and chariotry and great multitude'; one-half if 'the battle be strong' and the existence of the State in peril. These degrees of mobilisation astounded the Israelis because they corresponded closely with those put into effect two thousand years later on the eve of the Arab-Israeli Six Day War of June, 1967.

The Essenes are believed to have secreted all their scrolls in surrounding caves when their own peril became extreme in the Jewish rebellion of 66 to 73 AD and before the Romans took Qumran. In the fire-blackened debris of the ruins of the Essene buildings have been found tell-tale arrow-heads of iron which the Roman legionaries used.

War—but a final war on earth—dominated Essene belief. They were apocalyptics, men who saw mankind in the grip of conflicting forces, Light versus Darkness, Truth versus Falsehood, God versus Satan. Apocalyptics believe the sovereignty of God is the only hope of salvation.

Piecing together thousands of scraps of scroll was an extraordinary operation, for the edges of many bits had been eaten by moths and worms so that neighbouring portions did not fit exactly and the work took on the semblance of a vast jigsaw of nightmarish frustrations.

Part of a scroll hoard discovered in 1952, laid out for sorting and editing in the Palestine Archaeological Museum, Jerusalem.

But as more and more scrolls were assembled and read, more and more startling resemblances between Essene and early Christian theory emerged. The early Christians also had apocalyptic convictions, and like the Essenes they divorced themselves from the Pharisees and other Judaic sects in believing themselves to be elect people of God. Both Essenes and the early Christians believed they were living in 'the last days'. One of the Essene scrolls lays down that 'when these things come to pass in Israel to the Community . . . they will separate themselves from the abode of perverse men and go into the desert to prepare there the way of the Lord . . .' The Essenes saw themselves as John the Baptist saw himself. They quote the same words from the Book of Isaiah that the New Testament quotes about him: 'The voice of him that crieth in the wilderness, Prepare ye the way of the Lord, make straight in the desert a highway for our God.'

Both the Essenes and the early Christians put heavy stress on their belief in the brotherhood of man. Before one became an Essene one must give up all private possessions. Of the early Christians the Acts of the Apostles record that 'Neither said any of them that aught of the things which he possessed was his own; but they had all things in common.' One book used by the Dead Sea sect has this passage:

> 'I was alone and God comforted me. I was sick
> and the Lord visited me. I was in prison and
> my Lord showed favour to me.'

According to St Matthew, when Jesus was describing the last judgment he said:

> 'For I was an hungered and ye gave me meat:
> I was thirsty and ye gave me drink;
> I was a stranger and ye took me in; naked and
> ye clothed me: I was sick and ye visited me:
> I was in prison and ye came to me.'

In short, the scrolls revealed innumerable instances of common language, common doctrines, and common institutions in the Essene community and the early Christian church. But they also revealed many and vital differences. What distinguishes them most of all is the Christian belief in the birth of Christ as the Saviour, his exaltation and his resurrection.

Both the Essene people and the early Christians lived in the expectation of a new age when God would destroy all darkness and

One of the many pools
and reservoirs at
Qumran. It is believed
to have been an
Essene baptistry.

wickedness, but whereas the Essenes looked to the future arrival
of a royal messiah, commander of the troops in the final war and
king of a new Israel, for the Christians the crisis was already past and
victory won. Jesus the Christ has 'overcome the world' (that is,
the kingdom of the Prince of Darkness) and has been raised from the
dead.

At the end of time, according to the teaching of Jesus, God would
gather the poor and the lame, the sick and the sinner into his
kingdom, and because the 'kingdom of Heaven is at hand' he exhorted
his disciples to go out and heal the sick, raise the dead and cast out
devils. But the Essenes excluded from the feast at the end of time
all the unclean, and those mutilated in body and distorted in spirit:
they were unworthy.

But the greatest difference of all comes in Christ's teaching of
love: 'I say unto you, Love your enemies, bless them that curse
you, do good to them that hate you . . .' perhaps the most astonishing
commandment in human history. The Essenes were not so inclined.
Their rule required that one 'hate all the children of darkness'.

Cave 4 at Qumran in which thousands of scroll fragments were found. Most books of the Hebrew Old Testament were represented, and in addition there were fragments of apocryphal books.

The Teacher of Righteousness felt nothing but loathing for his enemies. Evidence from the scrolls suggests that in fact the Essene community sprang from quarrelling priestly houses of Israel and that the Teacher of Righteousness was no more than a priest himself, who ended up on the losing side and led his supporters into exile on the desolate shores of the Dead Sea.

Was there a link between Jesus and the Essenes through John the Baptist? Dr William H. Brownlee, a scrolls expert, thought that John might have been one of those 'other men's children' whom bachelor Essenes adopted and (says Josephus) moulded 'in accordance with their principles'. Did Jesus imbibe some Essene thinking via John? Jesus and John, according to St Luke, were relatives on their mothers' side, and Jesus came down, we are told in the Bible, from Galilee to be baptised by John and fasted forty days in the wilderness. The scrolls have not given answers to these questions. Jesus is not named in the scrolls and the Essenes are not named in the New Testament though it seems they must have been known to the New Testament writers.

What, then, have the scrolls so far revealed that set the scholarly and theological worlds in such commotion? The general, though not necessarily uncontested, view of scholars is that they have shifted or modified the old concept that Christianity came upon the world as a sudden and unheralded blaze of light. Instead the scrolls suggest that Christianity emerged from a great religious turmoil and that ideas in many ways similar to those of the Christian Gospel were current among Jewish sects in Palestine before and during the life-time of Jesus. Or as the Biblical scholar Frank Moore Cross has said, the New Testament faith was not an entirely new faith, but rather the fulfilment of an old faith: Jesus did not come to present a new system of universal truth, but to fulfil the past work of God, to confirm the faith and to open the meaning of the Law and the Prophets. The New Testament, Cross has said, does not set aside or supplant the Old Testament but confirms it and from its own point of view completes it. The lay writer, Edmund Wilson, has guessed that the Essene movement 'nourished a leader who was to transcend both Judaism and Essenism and whose followers were to found a church that would outlive the Roman Empire . . .' Indeed, he was inclined to believe that the monastery at Qumran, 'this structure of stone that endures, between the bitter waters and the precipitous cliffs, with its ovens and its inkwells, its mill and its sump, its constellation of sacred fonts and the unadorned graves of its dead, is perhaps, more than Bethlehem or Nazareth, the cradle of Christianity.'

One reason why archaeology in Palestine is now so exciting is the possibility that further discoveries—further scrolls—may confirm or confound such conclusions. Surprises still to come could be greater than those already made manifest. Frank Cross, finding lines of continuity between Moses and Jesus, Isaiah and Jesus, the Righteous Teacher and Jesus, John the Baptist and Jesus, con-cluded that Biblical faith is not a system of ideas, but a history of God's act of redemption. The Christian ethic of 'Love your enemies, do good to those that hate you,' is still, after its enunciation two thousand years ago, untried in international relationships. Perhaps it may still be the only salvation of mankind.

# BOOKS FOR FURTHER READING

ALBRIGHT, W. F., Archaeology and the Religion of Israel (The Johns Hopkins Press, Toronto 1953)

ALLEGRO, JOHN, Search in the Desert (W. H. Allen, London 1965)

Archaeological Discoveries in the Holy Land (Archaeological Institute of America, 1967)

BARBOUR, NEVILL, Nisi Dominus (George G. Harrap, London 1946)

BERMANT, CHAIM, Israel (Thames and Hudson, London 1967)

BORCHSENIUS, PAUL, And it was Morning (George Allen and Unwin, London 1962)

Cuneiform Texts (British Museum, London 1968)

BUDGE, W. E., The Babylonian Story of the Deluge and the Epic of Gilgamesh (British Museum, London 1920)

CROSS, FRANK, The Ancient Library of Qumran (Gerald Duckworth, London 1958)

FINEGAN, JACK, Light From the Ancient Past (Princeton University Press 1946 and 1959)

FLAVIUS, JOSEPHUS, Antiquities and Jewish Wars (London, 1754)

GADD, E., The Fall of Nineveh (Milford, London 1923)

GILBERT, MARTIN, Jewish History Atlas (Weidenfeld and Nicolson, London 1969)

KELLER, WERNER, The Bible as History (Hodder and Stoughton, London 1956)

KENYON, SIR FREDERICK, The Bible and Archaeology (George G. Harrap, London 1940)

KENYON, K. M., Jerusalem (Thames and Hudson, London 1968); Digging up Jericho (Ernest Benn Ltd, 1957).

LAYARD, A. H., Discoveries in the Ruins of Nineveh (John Murray, London 1853); Discoveries in the Ruins of Babylon (John Murray, London 1854)

MORTON, H. V., In the Steps of the Master (Methuen, London 1953)

PARROT, A., Sumer (Volume I ARTS OF MANKIND, Thames and Hudson, London 1960)

PARROT, A., Nineveh and Babylon (Volume II ARTS OF MANKIND, Thames and Hudson, London 1961)

PEARLMAN, MOSHE, The Zealots of Masada (Hamish Hamilton, London 1969)

PEARLMAN, MOSHE, and KOLLEK, TEDDY, Jerusalem (Weidenfeld and Nicolson, London 1968)

ROWLEY, HAROLD H., New Atlas of the Bible (William Collins & Sons, London 1969)

SALMON, EDWARD T., A History of the Roman World, 30 BC to 138 AD (Methuen, London 1968)

SETON, LLOYD, Foundations in the Dust (Oxford University Press 1947)

TODD, J. M., The Ancient World (Hodder and Stoughton, London 1938)

TOYNBEE, ARNOLD, (Editor), The Crucible of Christianity (Thames and Hudson, London 1969)

VERMES, G., The Dead Sea Scrolls (Penguin Books, Harmondsworth 1962)

WILSON, EDMUND, The Dead Sea Scrolls 1947–69 (W. H. Allen, London 1969)

WOOLLEY, C. LEONARD, Ur of the Chaldees (British Museum, London 1935)

YADIN, YIGAEL, The Message of the Scrolls (Weidenfeld and Nicolson, London 1957); Masada: Preliminary Report on the First Season of Excavations (Weidenfeld and Nicolson, London 1966); Herod's Fortress and the Zealots' Last Stand (Weidenfeld and Nicolson, London 1966). Bar Kokhba (Weidenfeld and Nicolson, London 1971)

# INDEX